A COMPLETE PROPERTY BUYER'S GUIDE 2007/8
BY DOMINIC WHITING

ORDER ONLINE AT

WWW.BUYINGINGUIDES.INFO

apogee *publishing*

3

Buyingin**Turkey**2007/08

BY DOMINIC WHITING

Ready and waiting: A new apartment complex in Side. Mecitoglu Homes, www.homeinturkey.com

BY DOMINIC WHITING

www.buyinginguides.info
Third edition 2007/08

Contributors: Ben Crawley & Kathryn Liston
Publishing assistant: Rebecca Capitani
Managing Editor & Publisher: Dominic Whiting
Sales Director: Luke Hope
Sales Executive: David Miaron
Design: Deniz Kutlukan & Özgür Ergüney
Photography: Dominic Whiting
Cover image: A villa in Akkaya, www.curbanoglu.co.uk

Published by Apogee Publishing, 70 Mornington Street, London, NW1 7QE, UK.
info@apogee-publishing.com   www.buyinginguides.info   ©Apogee Publishing Ltd. 2007.

Contents

Country Background

Buying Property

West Mediterranean

East Mediterranean

Property news, free online guides and e-shop at:
www.buyinginguides.info

Living in Turkey

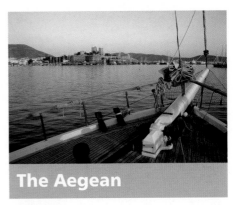

The Aegean

Cappadocia & Istanbul

Information

flagman&taylor®

agents•auctioneers•constructors

No. 1 since 1976...

www.flagman-taylor.com

Coast Park

Your Dream Home In Kusadasi Is Just a Call Away

PRICES STARTING FROM £45.000

Capital
DEVELOPMENTS & REAL ESTATE

Visit us on the web at:

www.capitaldevelopments.net

Kusadasi Office / Wendy OZDEMIR	Avril NEVIN / Dublin Contact	Mandy FLANAGAN / UK Contact
Phone 0090 256 613 37 08	Phone +353 87 122 08 07	Mobile +44 778 611 33 19
Fax 0090 256 613 37 11		Phone +44 1293 422 305

Country Background

History

Prime real estate: The Topkapı Palace in Istanbul was home to the Ottoman sultans

At a crossroads of great civilizations, Turkey has a fascinating history stretching back over 10,000 years

TURKEY AT A GLANCE
Area: 770,760 km2
(x3 larger than the UK)
Population: 73 million
Official Language: Turkish
Capital City: Ankara
Religion: 99% Muslim

The Turkish countryside is littered with hundreds of historic sites

At the eastern end of the Mediterranean, Turkey's pivotal position between Europe, Asia and the Middle East, has ensured it a long and colourful past. Some of the earliest human settlements grew up within the country over 10,000 years ago. At Çatal Höyük, near the city of Konya, archaeologists have unearthed a Neolithic town - some of the oldest known real estate in the world.

Since then, Anatolia - as the landmass forming the country is called - has been a bridge, across which successive tides of civilization have swept. The mysterious Hittites, the ancient Greeks, the Persians, the Romans and their successors, the Byzantines, all held sway over what is now Turkey. Each left a wealth of archaeological and architectural treasures scattered across the country. The awe-inspiring Byzantine cathedral of Haghia Sophia, the well-preserved Roman theatre at Aspendos, the Library of Celsus at Ephesus and the Hittite city of Hattuşaş, to name but a few. The Turkish countryside is also littered with hundreds of smaller historic sites too. In fact, it is often said that Turkey has more ancient Greek remains than Greece; more Roman ruins than Italy, making it a paradise for amateur archaeologists and sightseers.

In 1453, Byzantine Constantinople, once the wealthiest city in all of Christendom, fell to the Turkish army of Mehmet the Conqueror. As the new Ottoman capital of Istanbul, the city was home to the opulent court of the sultans, with its mysterious harem, for over 400 years. At the heart of a mighty empire, stretching at its peak from the Persian Gulf to North Africa, from the Crimea south to Arabia, the city was graced with mosques, palaces and castles, many of which are still standing today. Despite its immense size and wealth, the Ottoman Empire suffered a slow, inexorable decline, which culminated in its ignoble defeat in the First World War. The Turkish Republic was established in 1923 following a bitterly fought war between invading Greek forces and Turkish nationalists led by Mustafa Kemal. As the country's first president, Mustafa Kemal, who became known as Atatürk, or "Father of the Turks", began a series of ambitious reforms aimed at rebuilding the country from the ashes of the Ottoman Empire and turning it into a modern, western-looking country (see below).

RECOMMENDED READS
A Traveller's History of Turkey
Richard Stoneman
Turkey: A Short History
Roderic Davidson

Atatürk
Father of the Turks

Standing in town squares; watching as you arrive at the airport or visit the post office; even sitting in your wallet, the country's first president and national hero, Atatürk, is everywhere in Turkey. Born in 1881 in the Aegean town of Salonika – in present-day Greece – Atatürk became an officer in the Ottoman army, distinguishing himself in the bloody First World War battles at Gallipoli. Decorated and promoted, Atatürk used his position to organise a nationalist resistance movement to fight invading Greek forces and eventually

establish a democratic government in the new capital, Ankara. But Atatürk didn't stop there, as he wanted to turn the new Turkey into a modern, European country. Writing a

new constitution; setting-up a parliament; getting rid of the last Sultan; giving women the vote; replacing Arabic with the Latin alphabet; even banning the traditional Ottoman hat, the fez; he achieved a lot in only 15 years. However, many see Turkey's eventual accession to the EU as the ultimate achievement of Atatürk's dreams. Partial to a drop of the Turkish national drink, rakı, Atatürk died of cirrhosis of the liver in 1938. If you're in the country on 10 November, a minute silence is still observed for the "Father of the Turks".

Climate&Landscape

Kaputas near Kalkan is one of a string of Mediterranean beaches which attract tourists

From the olive groves of the Aegean to the mountains of the east, Turkey has a very diverse climate and landscape

AT A GLANCE
Highest Peak: Mt. Ararat, 5,166 metres
Coastline: +8,000 km on the Mediterranean, Aegean and Black Sea
Average winter temp: 13C- minus 30C
Average summer temp: 25C- 40C

Turkey's landscape and climate – like its history - are amazingly diverse. The country straddles two continents, with the narrow straits of the Bosphorus and the Dardanelles dividing Europe from Asia. Mountains cover much of the country, with the highest peak, Mt Ararat, rising to 5,166 metres in the east near the Iranian border. Mountain ranges flank the Mediterranean, Aegean and Black Sea coasts, enclosing a high plateau in the center of the country. Winters are severe across this central region, as well as in the east, with temperatures dropping to a finger-numbing -30C in some areas. With mountains and lots of snow, it is not surprising that there are some ski resorts open during the winter months.

At the opposite end of the temperature gauge, the country's southeast, near the Syrian border, is swelteringly hot in summer with highs of over 40C. However, along the Aegean and Mediterranean coasts, where most foreigners come to holiday or buy property, the climate is much more pleasant, with mild winters and hot, sunny weather during the summer. Temperatures climb into the high 30s in July, but there are often cooling sea breezes near the coast. Most rain falls during the winter months, although periods of crisp, sunny weather are common in winter too. Even along the southern coast winter temperatures can be surprisingly cold with the occasional frost and a dusting of snow on the coastal mountains.

LANDSCAPE

Large areas of the Turkish countryside are very unspoilt. Pine forested mountains cover much of the Aegean and Mediterranean regions, with olive groves, citrus orchards and fields of vegetables, tobacco and cotton where the land is flatter.

The country's best beaches are dotted along the Mediterranean coast, roughly from Dalyan to Alanya. Further north, the coastline between Marmaris and Bodrum has a series of deep bays and peninsulars. This area is very beautiful and is ideally for sailing.

The Aegean coast has some good streches of beach, notably at Altınkum and Çeşme, although being further north the season is slightly shorter and the sea is colder.

The Black Sea coast, Turkey's wettest region, is backed by thickly forested mountains, with dairy farms, tea-plantations and hazelnut orchards on the lower slopes. The landscape of Central Anatolia is made up of rolling fields of wheat and grazing land. The strangely eroded landscape and fascinating historical sites of Cappadocia, to the south east of the capital Ankara, attract tourists and a small number of home buyers.

Turkey is self-sufficient in most agricultural produce, exporting fruit, vegetables, dairy products and meat to the EU and the Middle East. A visit to any local Turkish market will give you an idea of the amazing wealth of what's grown in the country.

Perhaps best known for its Mediterranean crops, such as olives, tomatoes, peaches, apricots, melons and citrus, temperate fruit like apples, pears, plums and cherries are also available on a seasonal basis. Bananas are even grown along the sub-tropical southern coast near Alanya.

Fishing is an important industry along the country's 8,000 km coast, although it has been eclipsed by tourism particularly on the Aegean and Mediterranean coasts. Away from towns and cities most people still earn their living from farming and the pace of life in rural areas is very slow.

AVERAGE MONTHLY TEMPERATURES

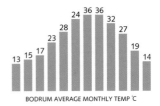

BODRUM AVERAGE MONTHLY TEMP °C

AVERAGE MONTHLY RAINFALL

BODRUM AVERAGE MONTHLY RAINFALL CM

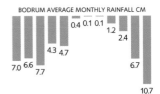

Rafting in the Taurus Mountains near Side

Culture&Religion

Islam is the national religion, but most Turks are moderate in their beliefs and the government is secular

AT A GLANCE
National language: Turkish
Other languages: Kurdish, Arabic and Laz
Religion: Sunni Islam, with a large Alevi minority
Population: Young, rapidly growing with +60% living in towns and cities

RECOMMENDED READS
Culture Shock! Turkey
Arin Bayraktaroğlu

A nation on football-lovers

Modern Turks are the descendents of nomadic tribes that migrated from Central Asia with their flocks over 1,500 years ago. The country also has large minority groups, such as Kurds, Arabs and Laz, who have their own distinct languages. Turkish is the country's national language and it is written using the Latin script.

Turkey's national religion is Islam, but the country is a secular state with religious affairs and government kept firmly apart. Most Turkish people are Sunni Muslims and they are generally far more moderate in their religious beliefs than people in neighbouring countries of the Middle East. This is particularly the case in the main cities and the coastal resorts. More conservative attitudes prevail in the less developed and eastern parts of the country. Women in these areas typically choose to cover their heads with a headscarf, although few veil themselves completely.

In the main cities and resorts most Turkish women dress in Western-style clothing. But outside these areas, visitors should dress modestly to avoid attracting unwanted attention or causing offence. Remember not to wear shorts or short sleeves when visiting a mosque, and women will need to put on a headscarf too. Alcohol is widely available in bars, restaurants and shops, and many Turkish people enjoy a drink.

The main religious holidays of the Islamic calendar, such as Ramazan, are widely observed in Turkey. Banks, government offices and many businesses are closed, and people traditionally visit their family and relatives.

Turkey has a young and rapidly growing population with 50% of its people under 25 years old. Military service is compulsory for all Turkish men over the age of 18. In the last 40 years there has been a huge movement of people from the countryside to cities, such as Ankara, Istanbul, Izmir and Antalya. Over 60% of the population live in urban areas, although their connection with family and friends still living in the countryside often remains strong. Turkish people are generally very friendly to visitors and there is a strong tradition of hospitality.

Turkey has a young, dynamic population, most of whom live in rapidly growing cities like Ankara, Istanbul and Izmir

Politics

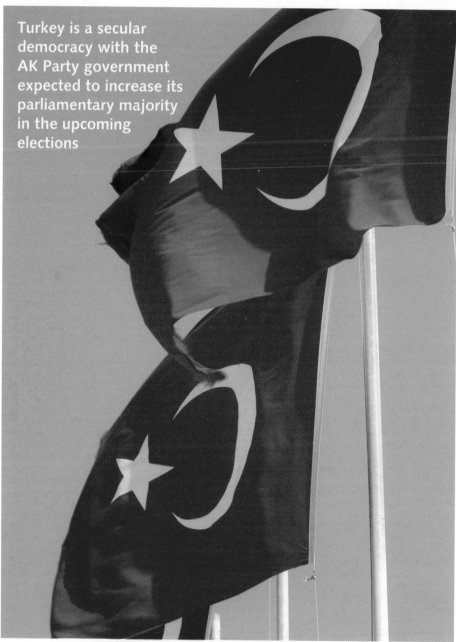

Turkey is a secular
democracy with the
AK Party government
expected to increase its
parliamentary majority
in the upcoming
elections

Turkey was ruled as a single-party state until 1950, when an experiment with multi-party politics led to victory for the opposition Democratic Party. Since then, Turkish political parties have multiplied, but democracy has been interrupted by periods of political instability. There have also been times of conflict, notably in the 1970s, between extremists of the right and left. The military, as self-proclaimed guardians of the secular ideals of the country's founder, Atatürk, have played an important role in politics. Coups d'état in 1960, 1971 and 1980 removed civilian governments and established martial law, although power was eventually returned to the politicians. More recently, the military stepped into the political arena in 1997, helping to unseat the pro-Islamic government of Necmettin Erbakan. Despite these interventions, the Turkish army is the most widely trusted and popular state institution.

The Turkish Republic has a secular, pluralist parliamentary system. Legislative power rests with the National Assembly or Meclis in Ankara, with 550 deputies elected every 5 years by a system of proportional representation. A 10% electoral threshold was recently introduced to limit the number of smaller political parties. The nation is governed by a Council of Ministers headed by the Prime Minister, presently Tayyip Erdoğan of the AK Party. The Head of State is the President, currently Ahmet Necdet Sezer, who is elected every 7 years by Parliament and who presides over the powerful National Security Council, made up of top members of the government and armed forces.

Modern Turkish politics has been plagued by factionalism with weak coalition governments causing instability and a series of economic crises. This came to an end in 2002 when the AK Party was elected with a large parliamentary majority. Despite concerns among secular Turks and the military about the party's mildly Islamic credentials, the government of Tayyip Erdoğan has introduced reforms that have helped stabilise the economy and which have enabled the start of accession negotiations with the E.U.. However, Mr. Erdoğan's nomination of his foreign minister, Abdullah Gül, whose wife wears a headscarf, to become the new president, provoked huge street protests by secular-minded Turks and veiled threats from the military. In an extraordinary move the Constitutional Court annulled the presidential vote, forcing the government to call snap elections for July 2007. The government is expected to do well in the elections and may increase its parliamentary majority.

RECOMMENDED READS
Turkey Unveiled
Nicole and Hugh Pope

Turkey
and the E.U.

Turkey became an associate member of what was the European Economic Community in 1963, although it didn't formally apply for full membership until 1987. Since then, many Turks have been frustrated by their apparent lack of progress, with Brussels refusing to set a date for the start of entry negotiations until Turkey had met certain conditions. Many of the recent reforms introduced by the Erdoğan government were aimed at meeting these targets, opening the way for the start of negotiations in October 2005. However, entry talks were partially frozen at the end of 2006 due to disagreements over Cyprus and though Brussels and Ankara remain committed to the accession process, there are considerable obstacles ahead, not least the opposition from member states such as France, Austria and new member Cyprus. Furthermore, opinion polls show public support for E.U. membership within Turkey has dropped from 70% to as low as 30% this year.

The**Economy**

Up, up and away: the Turkish economy has recovered well from a crisis in 2001

The economy is performing well with sustained growth, lower inflation and increasing foreign investment

AT A GLANCE
GDP: $358.7 billion
GDP (per capita): $9,047
GDP Growth rate (2006): 6%
Inflation: 7.5%
Currency: New Turkish Lira

The government negotiated a new IMF standby loan in May 2005, and remains committed to E.U. membership

Turkey has a very dynamic economy with a vigorous and rapidly growing private sector. However, the state maintains an important role in many areas of the economy, such as heavy industry, banking and transport. Privatisation, although a priority of several consecutive governments and the IMF, has been slow. Inefficient and badly managed public firms still dominate large parts of the economy and remain a major drain on the national purse.

The country's most important industries are textiles and clothing, employing between them over 35% of the workforce. These sectors also produce the country's main exports, although other manufacturing industries, such as car making and consumer goods, are of growing significance. Low labour rates and proximity to markets in Europe and the Middle East have encouraged the growth of these industries. Agriculture remains an important economic activity, employing around 40% of the country's workforce. Despite widespread mechanisation and large-scale irrigation projects, traditional farming methods and low production prevail in many areas.

Underlying structural problems within the economy, coupled with political mismanagement and global events, caused a series of economic crises during the 1990s. This culminated in a catastrophic devaluation in 2001, when the Turkish Lira lost 40% of its value. Thousands lost their jobs, while the country's GDP plummeted by over 7%.

An IMF-backed recovery plan introduced by the government of Bülent Ecevit helped stabilise the situation, although it was left to the AK Party government, elected in 2002, to guide the country out of its worst recession since the Second World War.

Fiscal belt tightening and economic reform have succeeded in cutting the public deficit. Inflation has dropped from a galloping 70% to 9.5% in 2006. A sharp fall in the value of the lira in May/June 2006 and high oil prices have kept inflation well above government targets, though this has had only a small effect on economic growth, which is forecast to remain above 5% a year until 2011.

Reforms in the banking sector have boosted investor confidence and the improving economic climate has promoted foreign investment, which should top $20 billion in 2007. The newly introduced mortgage system is expected to encourage further growth in the booming construction industry. Tourism continues to develop and the sector raised over £9.5 billion in 2005.

Despite these dramatic improvements there remain considerable economic challenges ahead, such as improving the country's tax base, cutting the public debt, reducing unemployment, which stands officially at over 11%, though is certainly much higher, and dealing with inefficient state-owned businesses. The government negotiated a new IMF stand-by loan in May 2005, and remains committed to E.U. membership, although the rapid early pace of reform has slowed with much of the government's energy focused on the upcoming parliamentary elections.

Traditionally an agricultural region, raising citrus crops and vegetables for the domestic market and export, the local economy along the south coast – the main area for foreign property buyers – is now dominated by tourism and construction. Fishing remains an important economic activity in some areas, while forestry and animal husbandry are significant in the coastal mountains.

The newly introduced mortgage system is expected to encourage further growth in the booming construction industry

21

The**Property**Market

The Turkish market is developing rapidly and looks set to attract a growing number of foreign property buyers

In the last five years Turkey has been transformed from a fringe destination for adventurous buyers to one of the most popular emerging property markets. Over $2 billion was invested in Turkish real estate from abroad last year with this figure expected to double in 2007. According to official statistics there are over 17,000 British-owned properties in the country, up from just 3,000 in 2003. All the things that make Turkey such a good holiday destination – like the Mediterranean climate, beautiful scenery, friendly people and excellent value for money – have encouraged unprecedented interest from holiday home buyers and retirees; while investors are attracted by the potential for capital growth as the country develops and moves towards greater integration with Europe. The affordability of Turkish property, with prices significantly lower than established markets such as Spain, continues to be a key attraction, but massive investment in infrastructure and leisure projects is also widening the country's appeal. Indeed, many of these developments are part of the Turkish government's ambitious plan to double the number of tourist visitors to 30 million by 2010.

Despite the excitement, a 6-month ban on foreigners buying property from July 2005 while the country's property legislation was re-drafted dented investor confidence and put a temporary brake on the market. In fact, the amended law, eventually unveiled in January 2006, has no effect on the vast majority of British buyers, who are concentrated in the country's resorts, and was aimed at stopping the purchase of large tracts of land and rural properties. A slow tourist season due to worries about Bird Flu and the football World Cup compounded the market slow-down leaving many properties unsold in 2006. Demand has picked up in most areas in the first months of 2007 and looks set to increase further, partly as a result of the new mortgage products for foreign buyers launched by several European and Turkish banks. But developers and private sellers eager to offload properties that didn't sell last year mean that there are some bargains around this year.

In general foreign buyers are heavily concentrated along the Aegean and Mediterranean coasts, and particularly the stretch between Kuşadası in the north and Alanya in the east. This area has the country's main holiday resorts, as well as some of the most beautiful scenery and the best beaches.

At a Glance
The Property Market

✓ $2 billion investment in Turkish real estate in 2006
✓ 17,000 British property owners
✓ 30 million tourists by 2010 (official forecast)
✓ 10-15% price rises expected in 2007

There are over 17,000 British-owned properties, up from just 3,000 in 2003

Expert View
Property Market

What does Turkey offer foreign property buyers?
The obvious things promoting Turkey are its beautiful coastline and climate, with great beaches, over 300 sunny days per year on the Mediterranean coast and pleasantly warm winters. However, the important thing is that all this is available just two-and-a-half hours flying time from western Europe, not a long-haul flight away. With more flight options throughout the year, this means people can easily enjoy their properties. Of course, Turkey also offers low prices, with improvements in build-quality meaning that Turkish property is excellent value for money when compared with Spain, for example.

What factors will affect the Turkish market's development over the next 3 years?
Turkey's rapid economic growth is creating a large domestic demand for property, which will be boosted further by the new mortgage system being introduced at the moment. The country's position as one of the world's top tourism destinations, promoted by ambitious government plans and infrastructure projects, will also have a positive effect on the property market.

Which parts of the country

"Turkish property is excellent value when compared with places like Spain"

would you recommend to foreign property buyers?
The Mediterranean coast is an ideal place to buy as the season is longer than the Aegean region and winter tourism is starting to develop with the emergence of the area as a golfing destination. Investors are flocking into the region and the tourism

infrastructure is developing rapidly. Istanbul has excellent possibilities for investors, along with the other large cities. Investors buying into the right projects off-plan can see annual increases in capital investment of 20-25%, or even higher.

Do you have any advice for people interested in buying in Turkey?
Foreign buyers should definitely appoint a recommended Turkish attorney who can speak their language fluently and who has a good working knowledge of the real estate market. They should talk to different real estate agencies and before they make a decision to purchase all documents, permissions and deeds should be checked by their lawyer. A draft of the sales contract should also be checked by their lawyer. Basically, people should proceed with a property purchase in Turkey with the same degree of caution as they would do when buying property at home. Of course, some parts of the buying process will be very different from what you are used to, but your solicitor will inform you about these points.

Utku Bayraktar is managing director of Flagman and Taylor,
www.flagman-taylor.com

Tourist development and building over the last 15 years have transformed quaint little fishing towns like Bodrum, Marmaris and Alanya into large resorts boasting modern leisure facilities, restaurants and nightlife, as well as efficient hospitals and well-stocked supermarkets. Large-scale projects, such as the golf courses around Belek, near Antalya, and marinas in Marmaris, Göcek and Fethiye, have added to the appeal for many investors and buyers. Those seeking a quiet Mediterranean retreat, however, may be disappointed by this transformation, but once away from the main centers, life continues much as it always has done.

The most popular places for British buyers are Kuşadası, Altınkum, the Bodrum Peninsular, Dalaman, the Fethiye area, including the resorts of Çalış, Hisarönü and Ovacık, and Kalkan. Further east, Side, Alanya and the golfing centre of Belek are also property hot spots.

The last 3 years have witnessed growing outside interest in property in Turkish cities, particularly Istanbul. Housing shortages and strong domestic demand have seen huge jumps in property values. Indeed, a recent Europe-wide survey by international accountants PricewaterhouseCoopers showed property in Istanbul is more expensive than Madrid, Stockholm and Rome. Not surprisingly, Istanbul has attracted the attention of both private and corporate investors, particularly as demand for housing looks set to continue expanding as the city's economy and population grow and the long-awaited Turkish mortgage system is launched this year.

Most properties in the coastal areas are used as holiday homes, although a small but growing number of people are choosing to relocate permanently to Turkey, tempted by the quality of life and low cost of living. Some holiday homes are rented-out when not in use, but the growth of the holiday rental market has been restricted by a lack of cheap, year-round flights and the dominance of the package holiday industry. The eventual arrival of low-cost airlines to the coastal airports (Easyjet started flying Luton-Istanbul last year and Sun Express have recently introduced a new flight to Antalya) is expected to boost the rental market.

There has been a dramatic improvement in the quality and choice of property available in Turkey. In an increasingly competitive marketplace, the best developers are offering high-quality property featuring cutting edge design and lots of imaginative features and great facilities to try and attract buyers. However, these improvements are by no means universal, so

PROPERTY HOT SPOTS
Istanbul: Strong and growing demand for housing is attracting investors and buy-to-let landlords.

Altınkum: A rapidly growing resort popular with British and Turkish tourists for its sandy beach. Close to Bodrum airport.

Bodrum: One of the country's most popular resorts, with interesting sights, good shopping and excellent nightlife. Beyond the main town are a string of very different, smaller resorts.

Çalış: Fethiye's nearest beach resort is attracting British buyers in droves thanks to some very affordable property and a long stretch of seashore.

Hisarönü & Ovacık: Set in lovely mountain scenery with the Ölüdeniz lagoon nearby, these two resorts near Fethiye are hugely popular with buyers – particularly from Britain.

Kalkan: An attractive, friendly resort with plenty to do in the surrounding area. The town has grown explosively in recent years.

Side: Sandy beaches and Roman ruins have made Side a popular resort. Now the area boasts villa and apartment complexes.

Alanya: A large seaside town with good beaches, entertainment and services. Wide choice of apartments and a large expatriate community.

TURKEY'S EMERGING PROPERTY SPOTS

Çeşme: Largely ignored by foreign buyers, this resort is very popular with Turks and has good beaches, world-class windsurfing and some attractive property.

Dalaman: A golf course is now under construction encouraging growing interest from developers and buyers.

Belek: Turkey's main golfing centre is attracting a lot of interest, and now has many new off-plan developments.

Ambitious development plans for the Dalaman area, including a new golf course, have encouraged major interest

shop around and do plenty of research. Don't be blinded by the bottom line – a more expensive property may be larger, better located or have better facilities, and ultimately make much a better investment. Also, beware of rental guarantees. Unless the developer has an agreement with a holiday company, this rental income may simply be added onto the sale price.

WHERE TO BUY

Çeşme and the Aegean coast to the north have largely been the preserve of Turkish buyers. Within commuting distance of Izmir, the country's third largest city, Çeşme is a popular Turkish holiday destination, which enjoys a buoyant property market driven by domestic, rather than foreign, demand. Although many properties in the area still offer excellent value for money, prices in the most desirable areas have sky-rocketed.

Kuşadası is a sprawling, rapidly growing resort close to the Roman city of Ephesus, Turkey's most famous archaeological attraction. Similarly, Altınkum has a good beach, plenty of activities and interesting archaeological sites nearby. Work on a new marina started this year. Both resorts have experienced construction booms and are particularly popular with buyers looking for the most affordable property, be it apartments or cheaper villas.

The Bodrum Peninsular is a diverse area with something to suit all tastes and budgets. Its popularity with Turkish buyers, some of them extremely wealthy, means the area has a wide choice of properties at all price levels, as well as excellent leisure facilities and services.

Further south, the large town and package resort of Marmaris boasts a marina and a sandy beach at Içmeler. The urban setting will not be to everyone's taste, although the surrounding countryside is very beautiful. Dalyan is a much smaller, quieter resort surrounded by unspoilt rural scenery, with a choice of villas and a few small apartment complexes. Ambitious development plans for the Dalaman area, including a new golf course, have encouraged major interest from buyers and investors. Despite rapid increases, prices are still lower than in neighbouring resorts.

Göcek has gained a reputation as Turkey's top yachting center and its most exclusive resort. Strict controls on development and a scarcity of flat land mean prices are high.

The town of Fethiye and the nearby resorts of Çalış, Ovacık and Hisarönü are one of the most popular spots for British buyers. There is a wide selection of property on offer, from town-centre

Now over 1,000 satisfied customers

Buying in Turkey has never been easier!

DREAMHOMES
WORLDWIDE

At **Dream Homes Worldwide**, we like to stand out from the crowd. Our properties, our services and our clients positive feedback is testament to how we look after our customers. Here's why we are different to the rest....

- The staff in our Bodrum offices are perfectly placed to offer local knowledge and expertise

- We guide you through the whole sales process and are always there for you

- We provide you with photo updates on the construction of your property and news related to your property

- We offer a FREE and comprehensive after sales care. It's all part of the service

- We are independent from any one property developer or builder and we only have your interests at heart

- We guarantee to show you at least 10 properties from 7 different developers during your visit to Turkey. Ask if anyone else can do the same

HERE'S WHAT SOME OF OUR CLIENTS SAY ABOUT US...

I would like to take this opportunity to say how delighted we were with our viewing weekend. There was no pressure at all and we ended up purchasing two! Illy was wonderful, an extremely knowledgeable and friendly chap. I would certainly recommend your company to friends and colleagues - I feel we have found the real gem in the crown.
Tracey Stewart

I am about to sign six reservation agreements relating to various properties in the Bodrum area and I have been delighted with the way that Dream Homes Worldwide have conducted themselves. They have been professional, efficient and friendly all at the same time in a way that has been very impressive.
Gary Copeland

Why not give us a call today and chat to one of our property experts about the

Turkish property market on FREEPHONE **0800 0193 847**

Alternatively, you will find out all about our properties and services at

www.dreamhomesww.com

DREAM HOMES WORLDWIDE HEAD OFFICES:

SPAIN OFFICE: Oficina 3.3, Centro Comercial La Alzambra
Urb. La Alzambra - 29660 - Nueva Andalucía - Málaga - Spain

BULGARIA OFFICE: Interpred - World Trade Center Sofia
First floor 332 - b - 36, Dragon Tsankov BLVD - Sofia BG - 1040 - Bulgaria

TURKEY OFFICE: Kemer Mah - Kapuz Caddesi 30A
48420 Ortakent - Bodrum - Turkey

Belek is the country's premier golfing area and offers a choice of apartment and villa developments

apartments to more secluded villas.

Kalkan is smaller and more up-market, with good access to nearby attractions, such as the beach at Patara. The resort has a particularly good choice of premium villas with sea views. As does the pretty seaside town of Kaş, although the distance to the nearest airport puts some buyers off.

Kemer is a utilitarian purpose-built resort set in some of the coast's most beautiful scenery. Favoured by German and, more recently, Russian buyers, nearby Çamyuva is popular with British.

Antalya is a large city with lots of modern apartments and some atmospheric houses in the old town. Belek is the country's premier golfing area and offers a choice of apartment and villa developments. The Mediterranean resort of Side has excellent beaches and historical interest, with a good selection of resale and off-plan apartments, though villas are more rare. Alanya is a much larger seaside town and package holiday center with beaches and lots of facilities, nightlife and shopping. Apartments, from luxury penthouses to budget flats, are most common, though there are a few villas away from the centre.

The historic cave houses of Cappadocia, generally hundreds of years old and requiring extensive renovation, are one of the most unusual property choices in Turkey.

PROPERTY PRICES

Prices in Turkey remain well below those in established markets, such as Spain and Portugal. Expect to pay £35,000-£90,000 for a new two-bedroom apartment depending on the location, build-quality and facilities. Villas range from as little as £45,000 for a basic three-bedroom house on an old complex, to over £275,000 in the more upmarket resorts, such as Kalkan or Göcek. Luxurious properties can also be found in Bodrum and Istanbul. For local prices consult our area guides.

Price increases in some resorts slowed or even halted in 2006 due to the freeze on foreigners buying from July 2005, however, soaring land values in the most popular areas will push prices upwards over the mid to long-term. Price increases of 10-15% are expected in the most popular areas over the next 12 months. But a large supply of new property in resorts like Bodrum and Alanya means the resale market is slow. Choosing a high-quality build in a good location will help you ensure the best chance of reselling.

The Property Market
What you get for your money...

£20K: One-bedroom resale apartment in Kuşadası
£29K: Studio apartment off-plan in Tuzla, Bodrum
£30K: Three-bedroom house in Akbük near Altınkum
£36K: Two-bedroom off-plan apartment near Alanya
£45K: Two-bedroom off-plan apartment in Dalaman
£49K: New one-bedroom apartment in Dalyan
£51K: Resale three-bedroom house near Gümüşlük
£53K: Three-bedroom apartment near Fethiye town centre
£59K: Two-bedroom apartment in rural setting near Belek
£65K: Two-bedroom apartment near the beach in Side
£68K: New two-bedroom apartment on a complex in Alanya
£74K: Luxury two-bedroom apartment in Yalıkavak, Bodrum
£75K: New four-bedroom semi-detached villa in Altınkum
£78K: Two-bedroom, two bathroom duplex apartment in Ovacık, Fethiye
£84K: Two-bedroom duplex apartment in Kalkan
£90K: Ground-floor duplex with three bedrooms in Sarıgerme
£94K: Large three-bedroom apartment with sea view in Kuşadası

Off-plan apartments and duplexes in Belek, £67,000-£111,000

New-build apartments with views in Alanya, £55,000-£90,000

A semi-detached villa in the Aegean resort of Çeşme, £120,000

A three-bedroom detached house in Ovacık, Fethiye, £139,000

£100K: Luxury three-bedroom duplex in Alanya
£115K: Three-bedroom villa with pool 10 minutes from Çalış beach, Fethiye
£116K: Three-bedroom semi-detached villa with pool near Çeşme
£120K: Four-bedroom apartment off-plan in high-rise suburban development in Istanbul
£125K: Three-bedroom detached villa in golf centre of Belek
£135K: Small three-bedroom villa with garden and pool in Dalyan
£139K: New 100m2 house with three bedrooms in Ovacık
£154K: Spacious three-bedroom villa with pool in Akkaya, near Dalaman
£175K: Detached three-bedroom villa with pool in Dalyan
£195K: Large detached three-bedroom villa in Ovacık, Fethiye
£225K: New four-bedroom villa with views in Yalıkavak, Bodrum
£265K: Five-bedroom luxury villa with pool in Kalkan.
£270K: Four-bedroom villa with swimming pool and sea view in Göcek
£350K: Large detached house with pool and sea view in Kaş.
£450K: Large villa with pool in a residential suburb of Istanbul

ParadiseFound

Anyone for a swim? Akkaya has ample space, fresh air and fantastic views

Stunning homes in beautiful surroundings, the unique properties in Akkaya are a great investment too

AKKAYA AT A GLANCE
Location: Near Dalaman
What's it like? An unspoilt rural area with stunning lake and mountain views
Properties: Apartments, villas and bungalows, available new or off-plan
Facilities: Swimming pools, tennis courts, shops, restaurant, on-site doctor, shuttle bus
Prices: £55,000-£158,000

DEVELOPER
Curbanoglu
Tel: 0845 355 5625
www.curbanoglu.co.uk

❚❚ We are creating a year-round holiday community in the most beautiful surroundings," explains Kemal Ilhan, director of Curbanoglu, the company behind a unique rural development in Akkaya near Dalaman.

The location is indeed stunning with villas scattered widely across a mountainside, amongst pine trees, olive groves and meadows, overlooking an emerald green lake. This is Mediterranean Turkey at its most secluded and unspoilt, yet Akkaya is just 20 minutes from Dalaman international airport, which is now served by year-round charter flights from the UK.

"There is no use having a piece of paradise if it is hard to get to," remarks Kemal. "The unique thing about Akkaya is the rural setting, but also how close we are to the airport, so you can be relaxing in your home within an hour of touching down."

Akkaya is also close to the new golf course at Sarıgerme and excellent beaches, including the turtle beach at Iztuzu, while the marinas of Göcek are only 15 minutes away. The surrounding mountains are perfect for exploring on foot; and the area's trails are ideal from mountain biking. There is fishing on the Akkaya lake or white water rafting further upstream on the Dalaman river.

Despite the secluded rural setting the facilities at Akkaya will be second-to-none with tennis courts, swimming pools, shops, a café and restaurant. During the season there will be a shuttle bus service to Dalaman and an English-speaking doctor on-site.

Property prices in Dalaman are low compared to other parts of the Turkish Riviera, but unprecedented interest from investors and foreign buyers are pushing them up fast. Government plans to develop the area into a major tourist destination will ensure sustained capital growth for buyers, while the uniqueness and exclusivity of Akkaya will add to its desirability and property values. Strict planning regulations ensure that the area will remain unspoilt. A maximum building "footprint" of 15% means that all Akkaya homes must be surrounded by large landscaped gardens, giving each property a feeling of privacy and space.

Akkaya is 20 mins from two of Turkey's best beaches

Akkaya has a range of new and off-plan villas, bungalows and apartments all set in pine forests and with sweeping views of the lake and mountains.

Lakeside Villas are three-bedroom semi-detached villas set in 14,000m2 landscaped gardens with two large swimming pools, a tennis court, a restaurant and shops. The villas cost £79,000.

The Whiterock Villas each have a private pool and large garden. There are three individual designs, each with four double bedrooms, three bathrooms and a guest toilet. Price: £154,000.

The Hills has luxury detached villas and bungalows with ample living space, three double bedrooms and large terraces overlooking a private garden with swimming pool. Prices from £132,000-£158,000.

All the properties are built using TSE (Turkish Standards Institute) approved materials and come with a five year construction guarantee. Personal payment plans and legal advice are available.

For more details about Akkaya or to enquire about a subsidised viewing trip call Curbanoglu, Tel: 0845 355 5625, www.curbanoglu.co.uk

At a Glance
Why Akkaya?

✓ Excellent value for money
✓ Close to international airport
✓ Near new golf course
✓ Fantastic beaches
✓ Beautiful surroundings

GettingThere

There is a wide choice of scheduled and charter flights in summer, with winter flight options slowly improving too

ENTRY VISA
✓ 3-month tourist visa issued on arrival
✓ Costs £10 for British nationals (see page 58 for visa and residency information)

WHICH AIRPORT IS CLOSEST?
Turkey is a 3.5 hour flight from the UK
Alanya: Antalya
Altınkum: Bodrum/Milas
Ayvalık & North Aegean: Izmir Adnan Menderes
Bodrum: Bodrum/Milas
Çeşme: Izmir Adnan Menderes
Datça: Dalaman
Fethiye: Dalaman
Göcek: Dalaman
Kaş: Dalaman
Kalkan: Dalaman
Kemer: Antalya
Kuşadası: Izmir Adnan Menderes
Marmaris: Dalaman
Side: Antalya
Cappadocia: Kayseri or Nevşehir

FERRY BOOKINGS
Alternative Travel
Tel 08700 411448
www.alternativeturkey.com
Or visit:
www.ferries.gr/mesline/
www.ferries.itgo.com

WHAT YOU NEED TO BRING YOUR CAR INTO THE COUNTRY:
✓ Valid passport
✓ Photo-card or International driving license
✓ Vehicle registration documents
✓ International green card (insurance)

Turkey is a three and a half hour flight from the UK. Turkish Airlines and British Airways have several daily flights to Istanbul's Atatürk airport, with onward domestic connections with Turkish Airlines or other domestic carriers to regional centres such as Izmir, Bodrum, Dalaman and Antalya. British Airways also have several flights a week from Gatwick to Izmir. Cyprus Turkish Airlines operate direct flights to Antalya, Dalaman and Izmir from Gatwick, Heathrow, Glasgow, Stansted and Belfast. Seats on scheduled flights can be booked directly from the airlines or through a specialist travel agent.

Low-cost airline Easyjet now fly from Luton to Istanbul's Sabiha Gökçen Airport, on the Asian side of the city, but onward domestic flight options are more limited than from Atatürk Airport.

During the summer season MyTravel, First Choice, Thomas Cook, and Thomson have charter flights to Bodrum, Dalaman and Antalya from regional airports in the UK.

Budget flights in winter are much more limited. Holidays 4U have a weekly winter service from Gatwick and Manchester to Dalaman and Bodrum with coach transfers to the main resorts. Sun Express have started a new twice weekly services between Stansted and Antalya and Izmir year-round.

Izmir airport serves Çeşme, Kuşadası and the north Aegean coast. Bodrum airport serves Altınkum and the Bodrum peninsular; while Dalaman is the best for Marmaris, Dalyan, Göcek, Fethiye and Kalkan. Antalya is the closest for Kaş, Kemer, Belek, Side and Alanya.

For airline contact details see the Directory on page 135.

DRIVING TO TURKEY
It is about 3,000 km from London to Istanbul with the exact distance depending on the route you take. The northern option passes through Belgium, Germany, Austria, Hungary, Romania, Bulgaria and Turkey, with a long drive still remaining to the resorts on the south coast.

Alternatively, you can pass through France and Italy, where there are car ferries from the southern ports of Ancona and Brindisi to the Turkish port of Çeşme. Ferries run throughout the year, although the service is very limited in winter. It is advisable to book in advance at any time.

Buying Property

GettingStarted

Careful planning before you start your Turkish property hunt will save you time and help you avoid problems later

Mortgages are now available for some Turkish properties

Before you start your Turkish property hunt you should decide exactly what you are looking for. This sounds obvious, but clearly identifying your goals before you start can save time later. Are you buying for your own use or as an investment? Do you want to build your own house, renovate an existing property or buy off-plan? Are you looking for a quiet rural retreat, a city centre property, a mountainside villa or an apartment near the beach?

The Property Market (page 23) highlights the most popular places to buy and the area guides in this book provide more detailed information about leisure facilities, beaches and local property. This is a good start but you should also read guidebooks and other literature about the country. You can find a wealth of information on the internet too. Visit the useful websites listed at the back of this book and join some of the online forums, where you can make contact with people who have already bought.

If you are relocating permanently you should consider renting first, so you can get to know an area really well before taking the plunge. Visit several areas at different times of the year, to get a real picture of what they are like.

The coastal resorts are crowded in the summer and there is more traffic on the roads. On the other hand, public transport is better, with easier access to the shops or beach. It may be harder to get around without your own transport in winter. Off-season some resorts turn into ghost towns, with many shops and restaurants closed, and fewer foreign people around to socialise with.

Many resorts have grown so rapidly that the basic infrastructure, such as access roads and storm drains, has not kept pace. Some areas may be flooded during the winter rains and dirt roads can become impassable due to the mud. A brief visit in summer won't alert you to any of these problems.

You may also need to consider access to medical care or good schools if you have children. At the very least you should spend a couple of weeks in the place you intend to buy, getting to know it and comparing it to other areas. You will also get the opportunity to talk to other property owners, which can be very useful.

SETTING A BUDGET

Before you begin looking for a property you should set yourself a budget. This must be realistic both in terms of your personal financial situation, but also with regard to actual prices. Don't set yourself the unrealistic goal of buying a luxury apartment with sea views for £30,000! Rather than wasting your time, consult the area guides of this book, which will give you an idea of current prices in each resort. However, remember that prices are rising rapidly in some areas, so these should only be used as a guide. Another good way to check prices is to visit the websites of local estate agents.

If you are buying a resale or old property it is important to include the costs of all necessary renovation work in your budget. Get a builder or architect to give you a detailed quote before embarking on the purchase, so you know what you are getting yourself into. Set aside a contingency fund to cover those unforeseen expenses that inevitably crop up. When setting your budget you should also factor in the purchase costs, such as legal fees. More details can be found on page 56.

ORGANISING THE FINANCING

Part of the preparation process is to get the necessary finance in place, so the money for the purchase is ready. Acting quickly is important as the best properties are often in high demand. Have the initial reservation fee or deposit ready – this can often be put on a credit card – and make arrangements for funding the rest of the purchase. Many people choose to re-mortgage a UK property, but mortgages are also now available for some Turkish properties (see page 51).

FINDING A SOLICITOR

It is advisable to have a Turkish solicitor look after your interests. Often buyers don't see the need, and many sales go smoothly without one. But there are many potential pitfalls in the buying process, which a solicitor will help you avoid. Having said that, merely appointing a solicitor is not enough. It is essential to find one who has experience of Turkish property law and who has represented foreign clients before. Be aware that British law firms generally charge a lot more than Turkish solicitors, and will probably sub-contract the work out to a local law firm anyway. The British Embassy has a list of English-speaking lawyers in Turkey on its website: www.britishembassy. org.tr. The Law Society lists accredited Turkish law firms at: www.lawsociety.org.uk/choosingandusing/findasolicitor.law

At A Glance
What You Can and Can't Buy

The property law governing foreign buyers was changed in 2005/6.

What you can buy:
✓ Property and land within a zoned municipal area, which means all cities, towns, the coastal resorts and large areas around them.

What you can't buy:
✗ Property or land in rural areas*
✗ Property or land within areas of strategic, military or national importance
✗ More than 2.5 hectares of land

*Foreign nationals can buy in rural areas by setting-up a Turkish company (see page 53)

Get expert help with your Turkish property hunt at:
www.buyingin.co.uk

New vs. Resale

New properties are generally better built, but resales may have the best location and be a good investment too

At A Glance
New vs. Resale

RESALE PROPERTIES

Pros:
✓ May be in a better location
✓ Often cheaper
✓ May have more character

Cons:
✗ Often need renovation
✗ May not meet new building regulations
✗ More difficult to sell

NEW PROPERTIES

Pros:
✓ Meet building regulations
✓ Better facilities
✓ More easily sold

Cons:
✗ Often more expensive
✗ May have less character

Building standards have improved enormously in Turkey in recent years. These improvements are due to tighter building regulations and a new inspection regime brought in by the government in the wake of the devastating 1999 earthquake in the Marmara region. More developers are now building specifically for the foreign market, while greater competition and more demanding domestic buyers have also helped improve the quality of construction and the facilities that are provided on many new developments.

Due to these improvements there is often a big difference in quality between resale and new or off-plan properties. The main reason people choose older properties is because they are often cheaper than new-builds. Built first, they may also have the best position, nearer the sea or with an uninterrupted view. However, even in the coastal resorts, most older resale properties were built according to local tastes. For example, they often have more rooms in a given area and may feel cramped. Opening up the space by removing internal walls can solve this, though you should consult an architect or builder before buying. Be aware that some older apartments and villas may not meet the new building regulations, particularly for earthquake resistance. The quality of materials and finishing may also be far inferior to new-builds, and older resale properties often need extensive renovation, which must be factored into your budget. Once again, a local builder should be brought in to give you a quote before proceeding with a purchase.

Although labour and materials are far cheaper than in Britain, the cost of renovating can add up to the difference in price between an old and a new property. Competition from new-builds may mean that you have difficulty selling an older property too. On the other hand, buying an older property in a great position and renovating it can be an excellent investment and is very popular with Turkish buyers in areas like Bodrum.

Apartments&Villas

A private villa with a pool is the dream for many people, but apartments have a lot going for them

Most Turkish people live in apartments but developers are also building more apartment complexes aimed specifically at foreign buyers in all the main resorts. These new developments are typically higher quality with more attention to fixtures and details.

Apartments are a popular choice with foreign buyers for a number of reasons. Firstly, they are normally cheaper than villas, making it easier to raise the necessary finance. They are also more convenient as general maintenance and communal gardens are normally looked after for you. Apartment complexes may also have security and shared facilities, such as swimming pool and tennis courts. This makes them particularly popular holiday-lets, and they can provide excellent rental returns.

Communal services and maintenance are paid for by a monthly service charge, which is set at the beginning of the year. Known as an *aidat* in Turkish, this monthly charge may also include the cost of fuel if the apartments have communal heating in the winter. There is often a caretaker, or *kapıcı*, living on-site.

The main drawback to apartments is that they offer less privacy and less space than a house, typically 55-125 m2. Private outdoor areas are often limited to a balcony or terrace.

Prices vary between apartments in the same block. Units on the top floors may have better views and sell at a premium. However, being on the top floor is very inconvenient if there isn't a lift. On the other hand, ground floor apartments may be darker and less secure, although direct access to a garden can add to their value.

Villas are available for sale in all the coastal resorts. They vary greatly in size, quality of build and facilities. Some are little more than concrete boxes, while other building companies are producing luxury properties with marble flooring, air-conditioning and infinity pools. Villas generally have a garden and offer a degree of privacy lacking in apartments. However, up-keep can be expensive, particularly if they are empty for most of the year.

Villas are also less secure than apartments, although property crime is quite rare in Turkey. Buying a villa on a complex removes these drawbacks. The property is looked after while you are not there, and you benefit from shared facilities. In some areas villas on complexes are also easier to rent.

At A Glance
Apartments vs. Villas

APARTMENTS
Pros:
✓ Normally cheaper
✓ Easier to maintain
✓ May benefit from communal facilities
✓ Better security
✓ Higher rental potential in some areas
✓ Communal atmosphere
Cons:
X Smaller living space
X Less privacy
X Limited private space outdoors

VILLAS
Pros:
✓ More living space & privacy
✓ Private outside space
✓ Good rental potential in some areas
Cons:
X More expensive
X Higher maintenance costs
X Less secure

BuyingOff**Plan**

Purchasing off-plan is common, but choose a company with a track record and sign a contract before paying any money

At A Glance
Buying Off Plan

✓ Thoroughly check all the project details
✓ Compare closely with other projects
✓ Have the contract checked by a solicitor
✓ Don't pay anything until a contract is in place
✓ Visit the site for a look around
✓ Check building progress regularly
✓ Inspect the property before making final payment

The buyer also benefits from any increase in property values during the building period

A detailed floor-plan will help you decide which unit to buy

Buying off-plan is popular in Turkey. As the name suggests, this involves making a commitment to buy a property that has yet to be built. Selling off-plan reduces the investment required to get a project started. This advantage is passed on to the buyer as a discounted price, often significantly below the market value of a similar completed property. The buyer also benefits from any increase in property values during the building period, which can be significant.

The decision to buy off-plan is based on information provided by the developer or estate agent. This should include details of the location; a site and floor plan; building specifications and information about the materials to be used, communal facilities and prices. There should also be a construction and payment schedule. Carefully compare the details with other developments. Some companies include balconies, and even internal walls, when calculating the size of a property, so clarify this before making comparisons between developments. It is a good idea to visit the site to check the surroundings before going ahead.

The buyer then secures a property by paying a reservation fee, typically £500-£2,500, and signing a contract. Do not hand over any money without having a contract in place. As with any contract, it is wise to have an independent Turkish solicitor check the document before signing. They will also check that the developer has authority to build on the land and that all the building permissions are in place. You should also check the service charges when the property is completed.

Payment is usually in installments due on dates specified in the contract or linked to the building process. This second method gives the buyer security, allowing them to withhold payment if work has not been completed. On completion, it is a good idea to personally inspect the property before releasing the final payment. As an incentive to finish on time some developers include a penalty clause, with payments made to the purchaser if completion is delayed. By law construction companies must give a 5-year guarantee on materials.

You should opt for a developer who has completed several similar developments, and, if possible, visit several for a look around. You can also ask the developer for references from previous clients and check whether they are registered with the local chamber of commerce.

A Buyer's Tale
Off-plan Heaven

Accountant Tania Ryan could never afford to own a property in Ireland like the one she has bought with her parents in Kuşadası. "It is like something out of a magazine – picture perfect with balconies and swimming pool, it is gorgeous," says Tania who lives in Dublin. "I could never afford to buy it here in Ireland – not in this lifetime anyway."

She first saw plans of the development at a property exhibition in Cork and was impressed not only by the villas but with the one-stop service that the developer offered.

She and her parents, Sean and Mary Ryan, flew over to Turkey after the show to see the site. They were so impressed that they decided to buy a four-bedroom villa with swimming pool off-plan. The property cost €170,000 and they paid a €5,000 reservation fee with the balance paid in stages as the building work progressed.

The villa, which was finished earlier in 2007, comprises kitchen, living area, three bathrooms, including one en-suite, barbeque and basement, which will be useful for storing belongings if the family decide to rent it out. They were given the option to upgrade various items, such as changing the kitchen worktops to granite. Outside, the views are across fields of olive trees. "The

"I could never afford to buy it here in Ireland – not in this lifetime anyway"

views are amazing – the whole development has a real country feel to it, yet it is only 10 minutes from the beach," explains Tania.

The 28-villa development has gated access, a shop, minibus service to the beach and town and a caretaker living on site. Tania says the buying process was simple thanks in large part to the property company. "They took care of everything, the contracts, solicitors, insurance and furnishings – they've even picked the light fittings for us now," says Tania, adding that furniture is much cheaper in Turkey. "It was a great comfort to know that everything was being done for us."

The Ryans love Turkey having

spent several enjoyable holidays there, and chose Kuşadası for its close proximity to important tourist sights – the classical city of Ephesus is a 20-minute drive away. With a large extended family, Tania says there will be no shortage of people wanting to stay there. Sean and Mary, both retired, spent a month there in the spring.

"All the relations are popping up now looking for a week or two," laughs Tania, who can't wait to see the finished villa for the first time when she flies out for a holiday in May.

Tania, Sean and Mary Ryan bought from Property of Turkey,
www.propertyofturkey.com

Cooperatives

A popular way for Turks to buy, co-operative developments are generally avoided by foreign buyers

At A Glance
Cooperatives

✓ Favoured mainly by Turkish buyers
✓ Often very cheap
✓ May be poor quality and lack privacy
✓ Renovation often required
✓ Can be in excellent locations

Cooperative properties are normally built closer together and may have less privacy than developments aimed at foreign buyers

Without a mortgage system the only way many Turkish people could afford a house or holiday home was to buy into a cooperative development. "Construction cooperatives", as they are officially known, are a legal entity that can buy land, build and act on behalf of its members. Similar to the off-plan concept, when someone joins a cooperative they make staged payments, often over many years. As a member they own a clearly defined part of the development and a share of any communal facilities. However, title deeds to the properties are only issued when the entire development is finished and the members dissolve the cooperative. This can take years and puts most foreign buyers off. Many solicitors and estate agents also recommend against buying into cooperatives because of the potential for disputes between the various parties involved (the cooperative, the builder and the land owner), and because construction costs can escalate beyond initial estimates.

These are not issues for concern if you buy a property on a completed cooperative development, where individual title deeds have been issued.

Indeed, properties on well-established cooperative developments can be excellent value for money. But construction quality is generally low, so get a quote from a local builder for any renovation work before committing yourself. Also, cooperative properties are normally built closer together and may have less privacy than developments aimed at foreign buyers. Rooms may be smaller than you are used to too.

On the plus side, cooperatives are often in great locations and have excellent facilities, which are paid for by a monthly or annual service charge. In areas like Bodrum some old cooperatives have become highly desirable, with wealthy Turks buying-up and renovating the houses. Wherever the development, your neighbours will mostly be Turkish families, which is perfect if you want to immerse yourself in the local culture.

Coops in parts of Bodrum have become highly desirable

Old Houses&Renovation

Old houses are rare in most areas but can be found in towns and cities such as Ayvalık, Antalya and Istanbul

Old houses are fairly rare along Turkey's south coast. Traditional stone buildings are expensive to maintain and impractical compared to the concrete homes that have replaced them. Unvalued and without any official protection until comparatively recently, many old buildings were demolished or left to fall down. In some areas earthquakes have helped the process. There are some notable exceptions where historic buildings survive in larger numbers, such as Antalya's old town and the Aegean town of Ayvalık.

Istanbul has many more old properties. The wooden houses, or *yalı*, on the Bosphorus are highly sought after and extremely expensive. Old apartments in the inner-city areas of Beyoğlu or Galata are more affordable. In Cappadocia, in central Turkey, people traditionally lived in cave houses, which have recently become popular renovation projects.

Buying old properties can be fraught with difficulties. They often have multiple owners, who must all agree to the sale and be present at the registry office, or have granted power of attorney. This can cause practical problems if they live in different parts of the country or abroad.

Before proceeding with the purchase of an old property have a builder or structural engineer check the building and quote for any renovation work. Despite low labour and material costs, renovating an old property is expensive. Houses over a certain age with almost certainly need complete re-wiring and re-plumbing and major structural work is also not unusual.

Your solicitor will need to check if the house is in a conservation area, or *sit alanı*. In these areas of archaeological, environmental or historic importance there are strict controls on any kind of building or renovation work. Your plans may have to be passed by the *Çevre Koruma Kurumu*, the government department that manages officially protected areas, as well as the local planning committee. Your solicitor will also need to check that there are no outstanding debts against the title.

At A Glance
Old Houses

✓ Old buildings are rare in many areas
✓ Have the property checked by a builder
✓ Get a solicitor to investigate the title
✓ Check if it is subject to conservation controls

> Houses over a certain age will almost certainly need complete re-wiring and re-plumbing

Old houses on the Bosphorus, Istanbul

Land&Building

Buying land and building is popular – though land values in the resorts, towns and cities are rising very rapidly

At A Glance
Buying Land

✓ Prices depend on location, land-use and building restrictions
✓ Title should be checked by a solicitor
✓ A surveyor should confirm location and boundaries
✓ Carefully consider what is around the plot

Your solicitor should confirm who owns the land, along with any land-use, planning and building restrictions

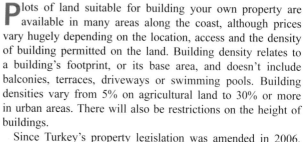

Plots of land suitable for building your own property are available in many areas along the coast, although prices vary hugely depending on the location, access and the density of building permitted on the land. Building density relates to a building's footprint, or its base area, and doesn't include balconies, terraces, driveways or swimming pools. Building densities vary from 5% on agricultural land to 30% or more in urban areas. There will also be restrictions on the height of buildings.

Since Turkey's property legislation was amended in 2006, foreigners can't buy more than 2.5 hectares. Land outside zoned municipal areas or within areas of strategic, cultural, historic and economic significance are off limits too. These new rules make land in rural areas out-of-bounds, although foreign nationals can set up a Turkish company to make the purchase (see page 53).

As part of the legal searches your solicitor should confirm who owns the land, along with any land-use, planning and building restrictions. You should also employ a surveyor (*harita mühendisi*) to confirm that the boundaries are marked correctly and the plot you are buying is where it is supposed to be. This may sound strange but it is not unheard of for people to discover that the land they bought is not where they thought it was.

When you purchase land you receive a title deed, or *tapu senedi*. This describes the plot's owner, its location with coordinates and its size as they are recorded in the land registry. The traditional unit of measurement for land is the dönüm, which is about 1,000m2 or 1/4 of an acre, but this has been officially replaced by the metric system.

Some rural areas haven't been surveyed by the *Tapu ve Kadastro Genel Müdürlüğü*, the government agency in charge of surveying. In these areas ownership is registered in a traditional village deed. Village deeds are legally recognised, though many solicitors warn against buying a property without an official deed because there can be difficulties when the area is surveyed.

Before buying land consider what is around it. If you are planning to build the person who owns a neighbouring plot may be thinking the same. Consider the effect of their construction on your property: will it overlook your house or block your view?

BUILDING

Before you can start building you need to get planning permission. This involves submitting detailed plans of your project to the municipal or provincial planning department. For this you need the help of a Turkish architect and a team of approved professionals. In some cases a geological report must also be commissioned.

Once you have received planning consent your architect can draw-up a schedule of works. This includes all the materials to be used in the construction, from the concrete foundations to the floor tiles and light-fittings. The schedule of works forms part of your contract with the builder.

Once this is completed you are ready to find a builder to quote for the job. Your architect may recommend a company, but it is wise to get quotes from several different firms. Seek recommendations from people in the area and also ask for references from previous clients. A contract, drafted or checked by a Turkish solicitor, should be signed by both parties before any work starts. The contract must detail payment terms, with staggered payments linked to progress on the building. A typical payment schedule includes installments on signing the contract; on completion of the concrete shell; completion of internal and external works; completion of the garden and landscaping; with a final payment held until any final problems, detailed in a 'snagging list', have been sorted out. Any amendments to the original plans or additional expenses must be added to the contract and signed by both parties. Building costs in Turkey are low, but standards of workmanship are generally below those expected in Western Europe. This means you should visit the site yourself as often as possible. If you can't visit regularly then find someone you trust to keep an eye on things or employ a project manager. Set a schedule for progress reports with digital photos by email from your builder. Some construction companies offer a complete service, buying the land, drawing the plans, applying for planning permission, constructing the building and even furnishing it too. This is very convenient, particularly if you don't have the time to make regular visits.

Depending on the project, construction can take up to a year. However, in the resorts a ban on building during the tourist season shortens the year by four months. Once the building is complete, your builder should get an *iskan raporu* from the local authorities. This is needed to get the utilities connected and shows that all fees and taxes have been paid and all regulations followed.

At A Glance
Building

✓ Get an architect to draw up plans and a schedule of works
✓ Have a detailed contract in place before work starts
✓ Pay in installments linked to building progress
✓ Visit the site regularly

BUILDING COSTS

Turkish construction companies can normally give you a cost per square meter for building in a particular area. Building costs vary depending on the type of terrain, the slope and the accessibility of the land where you intend to build. Of course, the type and quality of materials used in the building is also important. Extensive use of wood, stone or imported materials will substantially increase the cost. As a rough guide, construction costs range from £350-£1,000 per m2, with a small swimming pool costing from £5,000-£7,000.

Set a schedule for progress reports with digital photos by e-mail from your builder

A Buyer's Tale
Head Over Heels

"We were addicted to watching overseas property programs on the TV," laughs Stuart Hawker, a medical sales and marketing director from Northamptonshire. "The latest hotspots seemed to be Turkey, so I suggested we see what was on offer."

So Stuart and his wife, Shirley, an emergency theatre sister, visited a property exhibition in London.

"We were amazed by the number of developers building in Turkey," says Shirley. "We knew we wanted a two-bed, two-bathroom apartment on a small complex."

They also wanted a small town with enough shops and restaurants to give a holiday feel without it being too commercialised. One company was particularly enthusiastic and helpful.

"They showed us lots of examples of their properties - what was in the build stage and future developments. They also suggested the resort of Dalyan and showed us lots of pictures and information about the area," explains Stuart.

Totally unexpectedly, Stuart and Shirley found themselves putting a small holding fee down and organising a trip to view the area and proposed site. They stayed in a villa built by the company, which allowed them to see the quality of build first hand. They also met other buyers

"By the end of our holiday we had decided to upgrade to a villa"

and the feedback they got was positive.

"By that stage we felt confident about parting with our hard earned cash. We had also fallen in love with the area - and the rest is history," jokes Stuart.

During the building, the Hawkers were sent weekly photos of progress and email made it easy to communicate and keep updated. When the time came to fly-out in June 2006 to complete, the couple could hardly contain their excitement.

"As we had purchased off-plan it meant we had only seen a drawing of the apartment," says Stuart. "But we benefited from getting the best price and were able to

choose the kitchen style, tiles and other things."

The couple had "some issues" but these were dealt with over a two-week period and overall they thought the apartment was lovely. However, Stuart and Shirley also knew the developer was building some villas nearby, so being curious they went "just for a look".

"By the end of our two-week holiday we had decided to upgrade to a three-bedroom villa having been totally smitten by the area," says Stuart. "We're now awaiting the completion of our villa in June - we just can't wait."

Stuart and Shirley bought from Lycia Properties, www.propertyinturkey.com

EstateAgents

A good estate agent will help you find and buy the right property but you should choose the company very carefully

TURKISH ESTATE AGENTS

Whatever kind of property you decide to buy, unless you buy directly from a developer you will almost certainly use the services of an estate agent. A good estate agent has a varied selection of property and can provide valuable insights into the local area. Contacted in advance, they will arrange for you to view a number of properties in a limited space of time. But the services offered by most Turkish estate agents go far beyond those you would expect in the UK. They typically provide help with travel arrangements and residence permits, legal advice and, once you have bought the property, help buying furniture and getting the utilities connected. Many also provide a management service, if you want to rent your property.

The property boom in Turkey has seen an explosion in the number of estate agents. Completely unregulated until recently, many of these "estate agents" were driving taxis or selling carpets last year. Make sure that you approach a well-established company with offices and a track record of sales to foreigners. Don't make assumptions about a company based on their website alone. Ask for references from previous clients and check that key members of staff have passed the estate agent's exam. Since 1st May 2007 only qualified agents are allowed to perform property transactions in a registry office.

Reputable estate agents have also started organising themselves into local associations but there is no nationwide trade organisation yet. However, companies may belong to an international body, such as the Association of International Property Professionals or the Federation of Overseas Property Developers and Agents, whose members are bound by a code of conduct.

Turkish estate agents charge a set commission of 3% from both the buyer and seller. Developers often pay agents a higher commission for selling their properties. Unscrupulous companies may try to make far more by inflating the sales price, so do your research carefully and check what other agents are selling similar properties for.

Get expert help finding the right Turkish property company at:
www.buyingin.co.uk

Ask for references from previous clients and check that key staff have passed the estate agent's exam

A Buyer's Tale
Stress Release in Çeşme

Stressful jobs prompted John and Mary Woods to buy a villa in the village of Çiftlikköy near the Aegean resort of Çeşme. "We did not want anywhere commercialised. We wanted a place where we could retreat as we both have very stressful jobs," says Mary, an area trainer for Boots, who was introduced to the resort by her friend Sheila who has a property there.

"I fell in love with the place immediately. It was so beautiful and tranquil. The town is lovely, quite big and popular with Turkish holidaymakers but not commercialised. The bakeries make their own bread and the fishermen sell their catch at the harbour each day. It's a real Turkish community and the people are so friendly although we don't speak Turkish and they don't speak English."

Mary returned to the resort with her husband John, a construction engineer, last August. Having been introduced to a local estate agent by her friend, they were shown a number of properties in the area.

"Some we liked more than

"It's a real Turkish community and the people are so friendly"

others but once we saw the view from the roof terrace of the villa we eventually bought, that made our minds up," says Mary. "It looks out over Çeşme Bay and is absolutely stunning."

The three-bed semi-detached villa, which cost £75,000, was almost complete when they visited, so they were able to choose their own tiles, kitchen, doors and light fittings. Each of the large bedrooms has a balcony and there are three bathrooms. A fourth bedroom could be added on the roof.

The couple from Chester decided against having a swimming pool in the large garden because they are close to beaches and it is expensive to have one built.

They returned to England and arranged to transfer the 5% deposit to the agent. The

balance was paid in full when building work was complete and contracts were signed. "Everything seemed to happen very quickly then," says Mary. "The estate agent gave us regular updates as work progressed, emailed all the paper work and translated the contract into English. The whole process was quite simple but we couldn't have done it without them."

The couple intend to use the villa mainly for themselves but will consider renting it out to family and friends. They are planning to spend a week there in July and two weeks in August – and Mary will be going out with Sheila again in October for a girl's week.

John and Mary Woods bought from Villas in Turkey, www.villasinturkey.net

BRITISH & INTERNATIONAL ESTATE AGENTS

Turkish property is being sold by a growing number of companies based in Britain, Spain and elsewhere. These estate agents often offer a wider choice of property than local agents. They may have large websites listing dozens of currently available properties. If you haven't decided where you want to buy this can be useful, saving you from having to contact estate agents in each area. Some buyers also feel more comfortable dealing with a British company. Indeed, if you are buying through an agent in the UK, you may have legal recourse in a British court should something go wrong.

On the other hand, British or international estate agents, particularly those who don't specialise in Turkish property, may have less local knowledge of the areas that they are selling in. They may also have an incomplete understanding of Turkish property law. Finally you should check on the commission being charged by the estate agent, as this can be much higher than what you would pay a Turkish estate agent.

VIEWING TRIPS

Many estate agents and developers offer viewing trips to potential customers. These are usually 3-7 days long with the company typically organising airport transfers, an orientation tour and a series of viewings. Dinner and entertainment may also be laid-on in the evenings.

Viewing trips are a very cost effective way of looking at property, with the cost of your flight and accommodation subsidised by the company. If you decide to purchase a property, most estate agents will also deduct the cost of the trip from the price. However, remember that going on a viewing trip puts you under no obligation to buy. Don't allow yourself to be pressurised in any way.

DIRECT SALES

You can buy a property directly from the owner without an estate agent. In fact, this is very common amongst Turks, though you need to rely on word of mouth or the classified ads in the newspapers. Also look out for signs saying *"Sahibinden Satılık"* (For sale by the owner) in windows or by the roadside.

However, unless you speak Turkish or have a good Turkish friend, buying direct is difficult. There is also a tendency for the price to rise if the owner knows they are dealing with a foreigner!

At A Glance
Viewing Tips

✓ Organise in advance to see a variety of properties in different areas.
✓ Explain carefully to the estate agent want you do and don't want.
✓ Allow yourself plenty of time at each property.
✓ Keep a notebook with you to jot down your thoughts.
✓ Use a digital camera to take pictures of the main features of each place.
✓ Get a local map to mark the locations of the properties you see.
✓ Go back and walk around each of the properties yourself to get a feel for what the areas are like.
✓ Talk to other foreign property owners in the area.

Travelex completes the picture.

Using Travelex to buy your property abroad can save you thousands of pounds compared to your bank. Just imagine what you could spend it on.

Have peace of mind with Travelex foreign exchange. Contact us on 0870 010 0095 or visit **www.overseaspayments.co.uk**

The world's foreign exchange company

ForeignExchange

If you are buying a property in euros use a recognised foreign exchange dealer rather than your bank

In areas where there are a lot of European buyers, such as Antalya and Alanya, property is often bought and sold in euros. This means you may have to exchange your money before making the purchase. The Association of International Property Professionals estimates that 75% of international money transfers for property purchases from the UK are undertaken by the high street banks, with only a quarter of buyers going to recognised foreign exchange specialists. This is despite the fact that foreign exchange dealers offer a far cheaper currency exchange and transfer service. Not only do they secure their customers a better rate of exchange than the high street banks, but they generally charge no commission on transactions over a certain value either. Setting up a customer account is very straightforward and once completed you can buy and transfer your foreign exchange to a nominated bank account within a matter of days.

If you are making your purchase in euros, exchange rate fluctuations can have a serious effect on the cost of your property. This can be illustrated by looking at what happened to the euro in the first two months of 2007. The sterling/euro exchange rate went as high as 1.528 and as low as 1.456. This means that if you were buying a property for €100,000 it could have cost as little as £65,445 or as much as £68,680- a difference of over £3,000 in just 9 weeks! If you are using a foreign exchange dealer it is possible to avoid these fluctuations by fixing a rate for your currency exchange ahead of time – what is called a 'forward transaction'. A small deposit will usually secure you a rate for anything up to 2 years in advance. By doing this, you will have the currency you need at a guaranteed price and know exactly how much your property is costing you.

Most currency specialists also offer a 'limit order', whereby the client sets a particular price at which they want to buy the currency. The market is then tracked with the transaction made automatically when the predetermined exchange rate is reached. This method of purchasing foreign exchange is only suitable if you have plenty of time on your hands.

At A Glance

Why Use a Foreign Exchange Dealer?

✓ Better exchange rates than the banks
✓ Charge lower or no commission depending on the amount
✓ Avoid currency fluctuations by fixing exchange rate in advance

FOREIGN EXCHANGE SPECIALIST
Travelex
Tel: 0870 0100095
www.travelex.co.uk

A Buyer's Tale
Kuşadası Bargain

Sam and Denise Sameer were looking to buy an affordable villa in the sun. Even though the couple from Manchester spent £20,000 more than their budget, they believe they have got a bargain. The semi-detached villa on the Olive Grove development in Kuşadası is now worth twice the £45,000 they paid for it in 2005.

The villa has three bedrooms and four bathrooms - with each of the bedrooms having its own en suite with shower and toilet. There is a shared swimming pool which rarely gets crowded. Maintenance charges are £200-£300 a year. "The property was significantly cheaper than anywhere else," says Sam. "We'd been to Portugal and the U.S., but Turkey was more within our budget. Although the villa has doubled in value, we didn't go into it as an investment, we wanted somewhere to relax in the sunshine."

The couple started their search whilst on holiday. Although most of the resale properties they visited were cheap, they needed a considerable amount of money spending on them to bring them up to a decent standard, explains Sam. Whilst walking along the sea front one day, they popped into a local developer's office. "They took us around lots of property but didn't push their own development because it

"The villa has doubled in value, but we didn't go into it as an investment"

was £20,000 more than we wanted to spend. When we asked about it, they showed us where it was going to be built," says Sam.

The couple were so impressed with the development that they went away to think about it. "We decided to spend the extra money because the properties we had seen needed to have that much spent on them anyway," explains Sam.

They paid a deposit and the majority of the balance shortly afterwards. The developers took care of the legal process and all the paperwork including translations of the contract.

"It was such an easy process because everyone could explain everything to us in English," says Sam, an auditor. "All we had to do was sign the papers."

The couple could see how building work was progressing on the estate agency's web site. They even chose the furniture for the apartment on the web, so that it was fully installed when they arrived. Sam and Denise visit six times a year and have no plans to rent out the villa. "It is brilliant. The food is fantastic, everything is really cheap and the people look after you when you are here. We love the lifestyle."

Sam and Denise bought from Capital Developments, www.capitaldevelopments.net

Mortgages&Finance

Turkish mortgages are now available but the cheapest way to raise finance is often to re-mortgage in the UK

You have two options for raising finance for a Turkish property: re-mortgaging or securing a new mortgage against a property in the UK and using this loan to buy in cash; or borrowing against your Turkish property. The first option is often the cheapest as you can re-mortgage with few additional charges and interest rates for overseas mortgages tend to be higher. However, some people prefer to borrow against their overseas property so there is no risk to their property in the UK.

Recent changes to Turkish legislation have allowed several Turkish and European banks to start offering foreign nationals pound and euro mortgages secured against Turkish property. These lenders typically offer repayment mortgages of up to €200,000; or a maximum loan to value ratio of 75%. Loan periods are up to 20 years. Interest rates are presently around 6% for euro loans and 7% for sterling loans, fixed for one to five years. One major restriction is that mortgages can currently only be used for purchases in the coastal resorts and Istanbul. There are no mortgages for off-plan purchases at the moment either, though this looks set to change.

Turkish mortgages can be arranged directly with the banks, although Turkish lenders are not really set-up yet to deal with foreign clients effectively. Therefore, it is better to contact a specialist overseas mortgage broker who may have access to a wider range of products too. Brokers generally take an application charge, of say £395, along with a fee of 0.5-1.5% of the loan amount. Some estate agents and developers have developed relationships, or even specialised mortgage products, with specific lenders, helping their clients apply more easily.

The application process can be quite different to the UK and you may need a power of attorney in place to sort out property insurance and other legal requirements.

Don't agree to purchase a property or part with any non-refundable fees, such as deposits, until you are confident you can get a mortgage or raise sufficient cash. No matter how urgent the sales agent says it is, you should never part with anything until you have sorted out your finances. Remember that the penalty charges for delaying completion can be high.

Euro interest rates are lower, but unless you have a euro income you could be exposing yourself to potentially unfavourable changes in the euro/pound exchange rate with a euro loan.

MORTGAGES AT A GLANCE
Typical Interest Rate:
7% Pound, 6% Euro
Maximum Loan: €200,000
Maximum LTV: 75%
Maximum Term: 20 years
Typical Fee: 0.5%-1.5%

MORTGAGE SPECIALIST
Connect Overseas
Tel: 0870 4286574
www.connectandprotect.co.uk

Turkish Mortgage Centre
Tel: 0870 7708022
www.turkishmortgagecentre.com

Mortgages can currently only be used for purchases in the main coastal resorts and Istanbul

The Buying Process

Buying a property in Turkey is a relatively simple process but it takes a while due to the military checks

Most people are surprised at how straightforward the buying procedure is in Turkey. Once everything has been agreed, a property transaction between two Turkish people can be completed in an afternoon. For a foreign buyer it takes significantly longer because of the need for official permission from the military authorities. Below is an outline of the main parts of the buying process.

PROPERTY SEARCHES

Your solicitor will need to conduct a search at the registry office (*tapu dairesi*) to confirm that the property belongs to the seller, or that they have the authority to sell it for someone else. They will also check that there are no outstanding debts or charges, restrictive covenants or pre-emption rights against the property. For both new and re-sale properties it is important to ascertain that all the appropriate planning regulations were followed and building permission was granted. Checks should also be made to confirm that the property is not in a military restricted zone or in an area where foreigners are forbidden to buy under the recently introduced property law. You can also check on the status of adjoining land, if you are concerned about future development. In normal circumstances all the searches and checks should take no longer than 3-4 working days.

DEPOSIT & CONTRACT

After the initial searches have been completed, it is normal to pay a 10-15% deposit to hold the property during the military investigation process (see below). Payment of the deposit should be recorded in a contract, written in Turkish and translated into English, which is signed by both the buyer and the seller. Also in the contract will be the agreed price and, possibly, details of how the payment is to be made. Provisions for what happens in the event that the purchase does not go through should also be included in the document, which should be drafted by a Turkish solicitor experienced in property law. Contracts for off-plan

A Turkish title deed or *tapu senedi*

purchases (see page 38) also contain other details, such as the payment schedule, the date of completion, a schedule of works and any guarantees.

MILITARY PERMISSION

Foreigners buying property in Turkey must still be approved by the military authorities, despite a change in legislation in 2006, which should have removed this requirement. Until the new law is implemented permission for a sale to proceed is granted once background checks have been made at the regional military headquarters. These include checking for a record of serious criminal or terrorist activity. Minor offences should not count against you.

As part of the military permission process, the authorities also check that the property is not in a military restricted zone or an area which foreigners are forbidden to buy in. These areas are dotted across the country and may include land near military bases, along with areas of historic, economic or archaeological importance.

The military investigation should take 1-3 months, although unlucky buyers have experiences delays of up to 6 months in some areas. The eventual implementation of the reformed property law and a new computerised land registry system should drastically cut application times or remove the need for military permission at all. But it is not clear when this will happen.

COMPLETION

Once you have received the go-ahead from the military authorities you can proceed with the actual transaction. This is usually conducted in the local land registry office (*tapu dairesi*), although you can also perform the transaction in a Notary Public, in which case the title deeds for the property are officially changed in the land registry at a later time.

Performed in the presence of a land registry official, the transaction involves the current title deed holder, or their legal representative, giving consent for a new title deed (*tapu*) to be issued in the buyer's name. By this point the money for the transaction may have already changed hands (see below). An interpreter should be present to translate during the entire procedure, so you understand exactly what is going on.

As the legal owner, your name and details will now be on the title deed, a copy of which will be given to you. Additional copies of the title deed can be ordered from the registry office for a small fee.

SETTING UP A TURKISH LIMITED COMPANY

Foreign nationals can buy property using a Turkish limited company set-up for the purpose. One advantage of buying through a company is that you avoid the time consuming military investigation procedure. It also means you can purchase land or property in rural areas. A Turkish solicitor can help you establish the company with set-up costs of about £1,500. There are also administration costs, like a fee for preparing the end of year accounts. This option makes particular sense if you are planning to let the property, as you can benefit from the lower Turkish corporate tax rate and be able to off-set set-up and running costs against any profit. Thanks to a recent change in British tax legislation you will no longer have to pay tax on the value of any time you use the property, which until recently was treated as a benefit in kind by the Inland Revenue.

Under no circumstances should you hand over any money without having a legal agreement in place

DECLARED VALUE VS. MARKET VALUE

You may notice that the value of the property on the official title deed, or *tapu*, is lower than the actual price you paid for the property. Although illegal, such under-reporting is a common practice, which reduces the stamp duty and annual property tax. However, be aware that the government is slowly cracking down, and having under-reported the value of your property you will show a greater capital gain when you come to sell it, thereby landing yourself with a larger tax bill.

TRANSFERING THE MONEY

There are several options for transferring money to Turkey, aside from a briefcase full of cash (not recommended!). The best way is to open a Turkish bank account well before the date of completion.

You can then transfer the funds for the purchase from your account in the UK by Priority Payment electronic transfer. You will need to go into your local branch and fill out a form, giving the name and address of the bank where the account is held; the International Bank Account number (IBAN); as well as the account number and branch sort code. This transfer method costs about £25 and takes 3-5 working days, though sometimes longer.

Then you will need to arrange for the cash to be available at the branch or for a transfer to be made to the seller's bank account on the day of completion. The transfer of title will not usually take place until the cleared funds are in the seller's account or the cash has been handed over, though this depends.

Another alternative is to have your bank issue a banker's draft, a form of cheque, which can be sent by courier or even taken in person to the beneficiary. Remember that banker's drafts take

Expert View
Buyers and the Law

Why should foreign buyers use an independent solicitor when purchasing property in Turkey?
Foreign buyers generally do not have an understanding of the Turkish legal system and the numerous parties involved in the buying process. So like anywhere else in the world, a lawyer should be used to follow the whole transaction through. A good lawyer can help avoid the buying process turning into a nightmare. Companies and individuals involved in the property industry have varying levels of professionalism. A lawyer will look after their client's

interests and help deal with the seller, estate agent or developer.
However, appointing the right lawyer is also important, so check their previous experience and expertise. Remember that successful conveyancing requires the lawyer to understand their client's concerns, not just the Turkish legal system. To do this they will need experience of dealing with foreign buyers specifically.

Are there any specific considerations when buying off-plan property or land?

We are seeing more and more off-plan purchases. It is very important to make sure that the contracts between the seller, developer and landowner are established correctly. If this contractual relationship is not established right it can have undesirable effects on the buyer. Indeed, all contracts should definitely be reviewed by a solicitor before going ahead with any off-plan purchase. No money should be paid before these checks are complete and some form of contract has been put in place.
When buying land it is important to confirm the

time to clear once they have been paid into the beneficiaries account, so give yourself plenty of time.

If you are buying your property in a foreign currency, such as euros, contact a recognised foreign exchange dealer (see page 49), who provide a better exchange rate and charge less commission than the high-street banks.

Remember to transfer enough money to cover the costs involved in the purchase (see page 56).

If you are buying in a foreign currency remember to use a recognised foreign exchange dealer

OBTAINING A TAX NUMBER

Once you have purchased a property you need to register with the local tax office who will issue you with a tax identification number. Your solicitor or estate agent can do this for you following the exchange of title.

GRANTING POWER OF ATTORNEY

Granting power of attorney to your solicitor or another trusted person allows them to act on your behalf. This can be particularly useful if you don't have the time to return to Turkey during the buying process. It also saves you money on air travel and accommodation. A power of attorney can be drafted by a

zoning status as land in areas that haven't been officially zoned, such as most rural areas, cannot be purchased by foreign people. I advise any person planning to purchase land to have full legal checks made before making any payments.

Finally, is there anything that buyers and investors should be particularly wary or careful of?
Almost all horror stories we hear about have one common cause: proper due diligence was not carried out. For safe purchasing in Turkey proper checks, a well-drafted contract

"All contracts should be reviewed by a solicitor before going ahead with any purchase"

and follow ups during the whole transaction process are required. All documentation should also be carefully checked by a solicitor. In order to avoid any taxation issues, the purchaser should make sure that the registered value on the title deeds matches the purchase price. Under declaration is very common in Turkey but can have serious consequences in years to come.

Ayşe Özcan is a Turkish lawyer and partner of Anglo-Turkish law firm Acacia International, www.acacia-int.com
Tel: 0207 6103333

Turkish solicitor and needs to be notarised in your presence at the Notary Public. A power of attorney can also be drafted by a British solicitor, although it will then need to be ratified by the Foreign and Commonwealth Office before being sent to Turkey. This is a simple process but takes significantly longer than using a local solicitor. Turkish solicitors may also be more familiar with the various types of power of attorney that are required.

BUYING COSTS

The costs of buying a property in Turkey are lower than in the UK, but you should allow for about 5-7% of the purchase price. The main costs include a transfer tax of 3%, based on the declared value of the property. This is usually shared equally by the buyer and seller, although a different arrangement can be made and set down in the contract.

The costs of buying a property in Turkey are lower than in the UK, but you should allow for about 5-7% of the purchase price.

A registration fee, also based on the value of the property, is paid by the purchaser when the deeds are transferred at the registry office. If you use a Notary Public, the fees are standard and vary from £100-£250 depending on the service provided.

If the sale was organised by an estate agent their standard commission is 3% from both the buyer and the seller. This commission may be open to negotiation in some circumstances. Value added tax, or KDV in Turkish, only applies to properties bought at auction. You must also pay for compulsory earthquake insurance, which is about £35. Finally, don't forget to take into account your legal fees, which vary depending on the complexity of the conveyancing process and the property's location. Turkish solicitors typically charge £400-£600 for title and contract checks; British firms may charge much higher rates and generally sub-contract the work to a local Turkish solicitor anyway.

Living in Turkey

Visas&Working

For short stays all you need is a tourist visa, but if you plan to stay longer apply for a residence permit

At A Glance
Residence Permits

What you need to apply for a residence permit

√ 3 x application forms
√ An application letter
√ 6 x recent passport photographs
√ Your passport
√ Your property deeds (tapu)
√ A notarized copy of you property deeds

Residence Permit Fees

1 year: £200
5 years: £960
Plus £30 permit book fee
Note: charges may be subject to change

If you plan to stay in the country for long periods you can apply for a residence permit

If you are only visiting Turkey for short periods then you only need a tourist visa, which is issued when you arrive and is valid for three months. During this time you can come and go as often as you like. A tourist visa for British citizens is currently £10, which is paid in cash before going through passport control. Visa requirements for other nationalities can be found at: www.mfa.gov.tr/MFA/ConsularInformation/ForForeigners

Many people who want to stay longer than three months simply leave and re-enter the country on a new tourist visa. This is simple in many of the coastal resorts where it involves a day trip to one of the Greek islands. There is no limit on the number of times you can do this but staying after your visa has expired means paying a hefty fine, calculated on the number of days you have overstayed.

If you plan to stay in the country for long periods you can apply for a residence permit at the Foreigner's Section of the local police headquarters (*Emniyet Müdürlüğü, Yabancılar Şubesi*). In touristy areas the staff are used to dealing with European applicants, but don't count on anyone speaking English. It is a good idea to have a Turkish friend accompany you, or better still, your estate agent or a specialist agency may be able to deal with the application for you. Your application is forwarded to the Ministry of Internal Affairs (*İçişleri Bakanlığı*) for processing, which usually takes 2-8 weeks.

If you don't own a property or work in Turkey you can get a "tourist" Residence Permit, which is valid for 6-12 months and costs about £135 for 6 months, plus about £30 for the permit book. You will need to prove you have savings of at least US$1,800, or the equivalent amount in another currency. If you own a property, work or have been living in the country for more than 5 years you can apply for a full Residence Permit, which is valid for up to 5 years. This currently costs about £200 for 1 year or £960 for 5 years, plus £30 for the permit book. All fees vary for each nationality and may be subject to change. See left for the documents currently required for the two different types of residency.

You can apply for a temporary residence permit at the Turkish Consulate in London but once you arrive you must still go through the same process to obtain a full permit, so there is little point in the extra work and expense involved. A residence permit

A Buyer's Tale
A Long Road to Long Beach

Jeff Harthern from Crewe in Cheshire was no stranger to Turkey when he decided to visit to look at property three years ago. In fact, he and his brother had been coming to Marmaris on holiday for nearly 20 years, so he knew just what to expect.

"I decided that the time was right to buy a property in Turkey," explains Jeff. "Somewhere with a bit of space and seclusion that I could use for holidays, with the idea of moving out permanently in a few years time."

Starting in Marmaris, which he knew very well, Jeff drove to Datça, which he liked but thought was too far from Dalaman airport.

"After a long flight the last thing you want to do is drive for nearly 3 hours, so that was out," he explains.

Next stop on his journey was the Bodrum peninsular, which didn't impress him as much as he'd expected. He knew several people that had already bought property in Altınkum, but the resort didn't grab him either. However, first impressions of his final port-of-call, Kuşadası, were much more positive.

"It struck me as a really nice place and the property prices were another attraction too," says Jeff.

Having done a lot of research before the trip, Jeff had organised to meet estate

"It struck me as a nice place and the property prices were attractive too"

agents in each of the places he visited. He viewed four properties around Kuşadası with an estate agent who had responded to his initial email enquiry quickly and one house "appealed straight away". A three-bedroom, three storey villa on a complex of eight houses with a shared swimming pool, it is located in Long Beach, a quiet area to the south of the main town. He paid £31,000 for the property, which was at shell stage and still needed quite a lot of work. But it was finished off in a couple of months and he estimates the house is worth around £55,000 now. Jeff visits Kuşadası a couple of times each year for holidays and the house is used by

his friends and family too. Most of the other property owners on the complex are British, with several planning to relocate permanently to Turkey soon. Jeff loves the people and the slower pace of life in Turkey and plans to move out permanently at the beginning of 2008. He may rent somewhere more central when he does and plans to continue working part-time in the travel business using the internet.

"The pace of life is getting too fast for me back home and I value relaxing much more than I used to," says Jeff.

Jeff bought from Turkey Expert,
www.turkeyexpert.co.uk

Native English speakers are always in demand by private language schools

entitles you to live in the country but not work. If you intend to work or set-up your own business you need to get a separate permit (see below). To import furniture into Turkey you need a residence permit to avoid paying import duty, so this should be arranged in plenty of time.

WORKING IN TURKEY

Many foreigners are employed by Turkish companies or choose to set-up their own businesses. In the coastal areas most employment is in the tourist industry, although with the current property boom there are also lots of jobs in real estate too.

Istanbul has far more diverse employment opportunities and wage rates are higher. However, the cost of living is also significantly higher than other parts of the country. Other large cities, like Izmir and Ankara, also have a variety of jobs suitable for foreigners. There is a long official list of occupations that a non-Turkish person cannot engage in, including tourist guide and photographer. Work in other fields, such as medicine, requires special permission.

Native English speakers are always in demand by private language schools and some Turkish universities. A degree and teaching qualification, such as a TEFL certificate, is generally required, although some schools may employ you without. Rates of pay are low by European standards, typically £400-£1,000 per month, depending on where you are and how much you work. But the schools often provide free accommodation and flights home on the successful completion of your contract.

To work in Turkey you or your employer will have to apply for a work permit (*çalışma izni*). The application process can take several months, or even longer, but you can normally start working while the application is in process. You can also apply in the UK at least 2 months before your departure. Further information can be found at: www.turkishconsulate.org.uk.

Foreign nationals can set-up a limited company in Turkey, with or without a Turkish partner. Talk to a Turkish solicitor, or find basic information on establishing a company at www.hazine.gov.tr/realsectorleg.htm

GettingAroundTurkey

Low-cost airlines now operate between all the main airports making domestic travel fast and cheap

DOMESTIC FLIGHTS

Turkey is a large country and flying is the easiest way of travelling long distances. Turkish Airlines operate an extensive domestic network with flights from Istanbul and Ankara. Services to the main cities, such as Izmir, depart regularly throughout the day. Smaller airports like Dalaman and Bodrum have daily flights, which get very booked up. Turkish Airlines allow unconfirmed bookings for domestic flights to be held until twenty four hours before departure, so even if a flight appears full you have a good chance of getting on from the waiting list.

A growing number of airlines operate no-thrills flights from Istanbul. Flyair and Pegasus have flights to Antalya, Bodrum and Izmir; Onur Air to destinations including Kayseri (Cappadocia), Antalya, Bodrum and Izmir; while Atlas fly into Dalaman, Antalya, Bodrum and Izmir. Sun Express fly daily from Izmir to Antalya and other cities, so you no longer have to fly via Istanbul. Visit the airline websites (see right) for prices and online booking. Tickets can also be bought from travel agents.

DRIVING IN TURKEY

Thanks to major investment Turkey's roads, and particularly those around the main cities and tourist areas, have improved greatly in recent years. The intercity highways are now mostly dual carriageway and the main coastal road has been widened for much of its length, cutting journey times and making driving safer.

Even so, driving in Turkey can be a challenge thanks to bad road conditions and the poor standard of driving. Reckless manoeuvres, such as overtaking on bends, and speeding are common. Slow-moving trucks are another common hazard. Needless to say, the country's accident rate is very high. But once you are away from the main towns and cities, the traffic is light and driving is extremely pleasurable. Breakdown cover and information about importing your car is available from the Turkish Touring and Automobile Association (see the Directory).

AIRLINES

Turkish Airlines
www.thy.com.tr
Online booking available

Alternative Travel
Tel: 08700 411448
www.alternativeturkey.com
UK ticketing agent

Atlas Jet
Tel: +90 216 4440387
www.atlasjet.com/eng
No online booking

Flyair
Tel: + 90 212 4444359
www.flyair.com.tr
Online booking available

Onur Air
Tel: +90 212 6629797
www.onurair.com.tr
Online booking available

Pegasus
Tel: +90 212 444 0737
www.flypgs.com
Online booking available

Sun Express
Tel: +90 242 3291074
www.sunexpress.com.tr
Online booking available

HOW LONG IT TAKES...
BY BUS
(typical journey times)
Istanbul - Izmir: 8 hours
Izmir - Antalya: 7 hours
Ankara - Antalya: 8-9 hours
Izmir - Bodrum: 3.5 hours
Marmaris - Fethiye: 3 hours

SPEED LIMITS
120 km/h: Dual carriageways
90 km/h: Rural highways
50 km/h: Built-up areas

DOLMUŞ
Communal minibuses ferry
people around in cities, towns
and the countryside too. They
operate fixed routes like a bus,
but stop wherever passengers
request – much to the annoyance
of following motorists! The
destination is usually posted
on the front of the vehicle and
you pay the driver or his mate
when you get on. Dolmuş¸ in
resort areas like Bodrum operate
24-hours a day during the busiest
summer months.

FERRIES
Turkish Maritime Lines operate
ferries along the Black Sea coast
from Istanbul to Rize and back
each week in summer. More
useful for property hunters is the
overnight service between
Istanbul and Izmir each weekend.
This departs Istanbul Friday
evening, returning again from
Izmir on Sunday. Contact a
Turkish Maritime Lines agent in
Turkey to make a booking.

If you enter the country on a tourist visa you can import a car
and drive it for only six months in any calendar year. Details of
the car will be entered in your passport. If you want to leave the
country without the car it must be left with the local customs
office. You will be charged a daily parking fee for the privilege.

To import a car you need your driving license, the registration
documents and an international green card from your insurance
company. Long-term residents with a residence permit can re-
register their car and get a Turkish number plate. To do this you
need a letter of guarantee from a bank, a valid residence permit
and a work permit. For full details visit the Turkish Touring and
Automobile Association website: www.turing.org.tr. There are
agents who can make the application for you, and their small
commission is money well spent.

Foreigners can buy cars in Turkey but prices for new and
second hand vehicles are generally the same or slightly higher
than in the UK. It is more economical to opt for a car that is
manufactured in Turkey, such as Renault, as the parts are cheaper
and more widely available. Petrol is very expensive in Turkey
(see page 63), so running a car is a significant cost.

BUSES

Turkey has an efficient private bus network with modern buses
running between towns and cities across the country. As many
people still can't afford a car, buses provide the main form of
long distance transport and are very reasonably priced. Buses
are generally air-conditioned and passengers are served hot and
cold drinks. Smoking is not permitted anymore, although buses
make regular stops. Longer journeys can be made overnight,
although travelling by train or plane is more comfortable.

On most routes you will have a choice of companies,
including the premium carriers Varan and Ulusoy. Journey times
are significantly longer by bus than car (see left).

TRAINS

Turkish trains, except for the modern expresses between Istanbul
and Ankara, are slow and frequently late. But they are the most
comfortable and fun way of travelling long distances in Turkey.
Run by the state-owned TCDD, the train network only gives
scant coverage of the country, with no line along the western
Mediterranean or Aegean coasts. The only routes that are useful
for property buyers are from Istanbul's Haydarpaşa station to
Ankara, and then Kayseri for Cappadocia. There is also a good
overnight express between Ankara and Izmir.

CostofLiving&Money

Your money will go a long way in Turkey, although petrol, mobile phones and internet access are relatively expensive

The New Turkish Lira (YTL) replaced the old Turkish Lira on January 1, 2005. In the process six zeros were knocked off, making things much less confusing for foreign visitors. The old notes are no longer legal tender but can still be exchanged at banks. The New Turkish Lira has remained comparatively stable against other major currencies since a slip in value in May 2006, with £1 currently worth about 2.6 YTL.

The cost of living in Turkey is significantly lower than in Britain and other Mediterranean countries like Spain and Greece. Food and other consumables are much cheaper, while fresh produce is often grown locally and costs a fraction of what it does in the UK. Wage rates are very low in Turkey compared with Britain. A manual worker earns about £150 a month, while a school teacher takes home about £300. Baring this in mind, it is easy to understand why even a modest UK pension or savings can support a good standard of living.

There are marked differences in the cost of living across the country though. Istanbul is the most expensive place to live, but the cost of living is also high by Turkish standards in the coastal resorts. But even in these areas you can dine for £10-£15 per head in a good restaurant, or eat for a fraction of that amount in a local Turkish eatery. A typical weekly shopping bill for two is £50-£60, or more if you buy expensive imported goods.

One of the things that is expensive in Turkey is petrol. A litre of unleaded petrol is about £1.10, compared to 90p in the UK. Owning a car is a major expense and one that may not be necessary if you only use your property for holidays as public transport is so good.

Bills for telephones, mobile phones and internet access can be surprisingly high and in some cases you will pay more than you would in the UK. For example, a 1Mbps ADSL connection currently costs £36 per month, 3 times what you would pay in the UK. International call rates are also high, but discount call cards are now available in the main cities, or if you have a broadband connection you can use internet telephony software, such as Skype (www.skype.com).

TYPICAL TURKISH PRICES

A loaf of bread	**20p**
1 kilogram of tomatoes	**50p**
330ml can of beer	**50p**
1 litre of milk	**45p**
1 L of unleaded petrol	**£1.20**

Exchange Rate
£1 = 2.6 YTL
€1 = 1.8 YTL
Correct at time of going to press

Dining out is far cheaper in Turkey

Banks

Banking is simple in Turkey particularly if you have an internet
account so you can complete transactions online

At A Glance
Opening an
Account

**To open a bank account
you will need the
following:**
✓ Passport or photo-ID
✓ Proof of your Turkish
address, such as a utility bill
✓ A tax number from the
local tax office

Interest rates
have dropped in
recent years, but
Turkish Lira deposit
accounts still give
a good return,
currently around
15%

The banking system has recently been reformed but at the
customer level red tape is worse than in the UK. There is a
wide choice of banks with big names such as İş Bankası, Garanti
Bank and Yapı Kredi on most high streets. Before choosing
where to open an account ask for recommendations from other
foreigners. Bare in mind that small branches may not offer a full
range of services.

International banks such as HSBC have branches in Turkey,
but there is no particular advantage to choosing them over a
Turkish bank. Even if you have an account with the bank in the
UK, international transfers are treated in the same way. Banks
in the main resorts usually have some English-speaking staff,
although you may need help from an interpreter or a Turkish
friend for complex transactions.

Turkish banks offer a range of current, savings and deposit
accounts, which can generally be managed via the internet.
Credit cards and debit cards are usually available to customers
too. Interest rates have dropped in recent years, but the New
Turkish Lira deposit accounts and investment funds still give
a good return, currently around 15%. Alternatively, you can
open foreign currency accounts, thereby protecting your money
against any devaluation of the New Turkish Lira. Most banks
offer dollar, euro and sterling accounts.

Credit cards are widely accepted in Turkey. The Chip &
Pin system has been introduced so make sure you know your
PIN. Many British credit card companies charge you when
you use your card abroad, so it may be worth switching to a
company such as HSBC or Nationwide who offer free overseas
transactions.

Cash machines are found in all resorts and towns and display
in Turkish, English and other European languages. Foreign
credit and Maestro cards are accepted, but a fee is levied on
withdrawals. You can also make deposits, pay bills and transfer
money at Turkish ATMs.

Utility bills, maintenance charges and insurance premiums can
be paid automatically from your bank account by completing a
standing order mandate. Take an existing bill into the bank so
everything is set up correctly. Some bills can also be paid online
if you have an internet account. Alternatively, many people
prefer to entrust bill paying to a management company.

Taxes,Pensions&Benefits

Seek expert advice about the tax implications of buying a property in Turkey before you go ahead

PROPERTY TRANSACTION TAX

When buying and selling real estate, or registering a newly constructed property, a property transaction tax must be paid to the local authority. This tax is 1.5% of the declared value of the property and is paid before the title is transferred at the Land Registry.

PROPERTY TAX

An annual tax based on the declared value of your property and collected by the local authority. The rate varies from area to area, but is about 0.2%-0.3% for land and 0.1% for residential buildings, with the payment collected in two installments in March-May and November.

ENVIRONMENTAL TAX

This tax is collected by the local authority and is based on the amount of water used. This shouldn't be more than £100 per year.

INCOME & CAPITAL GAINS TAX

You must pay tax on any income, including rent, you earn in Turkey. Income tax rates are banded from 15%-40%. Complaints about foreign landlords not paying tax on rental income are leading the authorities to target foreign property owners in some areas. A double taxation agreement between the two countries means that any income taxed in Turkey is exempt from British taxes. You must pay income tax on any increase in value when you sell a property that isn't your principal residence. If you bought before 1st January 2007 you are exempt from this capital gains tax after owning the property for 4 years; 5 years if you bought after that date.

CORPORATION TAX

Turkish companies pay a corporation tax of 30% on profits, including those from rental income.

INHERITANCE & GIFT TAX

Inheritance tax rates are banded from 1%-10%, with allowances for the spouse and children of the deceased. Gift tax rates range from 10%-30% depending on the value of the property gifted.

TURKISH TAXES AT A GLANCE

Property Tax: 0.1%
Income Tax: 15-40%
VAT (KDV): 18%
Corporation Tax: 30%
Inheritance Tax: 1%-10%

Pensions & Benefits

Moving abroad will not affect your state pension payments, however you will need to organise for the money to be transferred into your Turkish account. Bank charges on relatively small, regular transfers can become expensive, so think about pooling the money and transferring larger amounts less often. A British pension can support a comfortable lifestyle in Turkey due to the lower cost of living. If you have not yet reached retirement age you should consider continuing to make National Insurance contributions after you move to Turkey. This will ensure you are entitled to receive a full state pension when you are eligible. Some other state benefits are payable to British citizens who move abroad, but you should check with the Department of Works and Pensions before you make any plans.

Services&Utilities

Getting water and electricity connected is simple, while gas and drinking water can be delivered to your door

Getting Connected

If you are buying a new or resale property water and electricity will usually already be connected. However, if you are having a house built or renovating an old property you may need to apply for new connections. This can be costly if you are far away from the nearest water main or electricity supply. To get the utilities connected it is essential to have an *iskan raporu*. This is obtained from the local authority and is only granted when it is shown that all taxes and permit fees have been paid and that the building meets planning and building regulations. The developer or construction company will usually apply for this, but it may be worth checking. When you take over a property any outstanding bills need to be settled before changing the electricity and water into your name. To transfer the accounts you need the title deeds or rental agreement, your passport and bank details.

WATER

Tap water in Turkey is chlorinated so it can be used for brushing your teeth, but it is not recommended for drinking. Instead you can buy bottled water from shops or supermarkets. Or it is more economical, and environmentally friendly, to buy water from a local water supplier who will deliver it in large refillable containers. Turks take water very seriously and people travel long distances to fill up containers at a spring that is particularly tasty or pure. Mains water is metered and bills are issued on a monthly or quarterly basis. Bills can be paid in person at the company offices, at some banks, or by direct debit from your bank account. There is a penalty for not paying on time, and your supply will eventually be cut off. Huge increases in demand have stretched water supplies and cuts are common during the summer in some areas. Some villas have their own storage tanks, or you can keep a container of water for flushing toilets or washing hands. There have been cases of water to foreign-owned homes being siphoned-off by people in the vicinity. Although this is technically stealing, it is viewed by some locals as a harmless "tax". Keep an eye on your water bills and report any large increases to your water company.

ELECTRICITY

Most electricity in Turkey is supplied by the state-run company TEDAŞ. The supply is 220 volts and two-pin plugs, like those in European countries, are used. With a suitable adapter, electrical appliances from the UK can be safely used. Like water, demand for electricity is growing so fast that the network can't cope in some areas. This means frequent black outs and fluctuating supplies. Apart from some candles, it may be wise to buy a voltage regulator to protect computers and other sensitive equipment from power spikes. You may also consider getting an uninterruptible power unit.

NATURAL GAS

Apart from in Istanbul, Ankara and some other cities with mains supplies, natural gas for cooking and heating water comes in metal canisters. These are ordered from a local supplier and delivered to your door. A full canister costs about £12 and last for at least 12 weeks when used for cooking.

Communications

Mobile telephones, widespread internet access and cable-TV make it easy to stay in touch

TELEPHONE

The Turkish telephone network is run by Türk Telekom. Getting a new line involves applying with proof of address, your passport and bank details at your local office. Bills are issued monthly and can be paid directly from your bank account by direct debit.

There are several tariffs available, with some providing cheaper rates for higher volume users. International calls are expensive, but you can buy discount calling cards. Try Superonline's Hasret Karti which are available from shops nationwide. For a list of outlets visit: www.hasretkarti.com/bayiler.php

MOBILE PHONES

There are several rival mobile phone networks but Turkcell currently provides the best coverage. Like in the UK, you can have a standard account or a pay-as-you-go line, with top-up cards (*hazır kart*) available in corner shops and petrol stations. You can open an account at any mobile phone dealer, with proof of address, your passport and bank details. Bills are paid monthly and are high by UK standards as there is no allocation of free minutes included. Pay-as-you-go lines require no identification or proof of address, but call rates are even higher.

You can use your British mobile in Turkey as long as you have international roaming enabled. British handsets can no longer be used with a Turkish SIM card without registering the handset with Türk Telekom. You will need proof of purchase, including the handset serial number, and your passport.

THE INTERNET

The internet revolution is in full swing in Turkey and there are wireless hot-spots in many hotels and public places. You can buy dial-up packages at branches of Türk Telekom or computer and electronics shops. A limitless dial-up connection costs £3.50 per month, or £21 per year. Broadband is available in most areas but is expensive compared to the UK. For example, a 256 Kbps connection is £18 per month, 1024 Kbps about £36 per month, plus there is a connection fee and you have to buy a modem. Apply at your local Türk Telekom office or visit: www.ttnet.net.tr

THE POST & COURIERS

The Turkish postal service, or PTT, operates post offices across the country and delivers mail. The service is quite slow with domestic mail taking 4-5 days, or 7-14 days for the UK. Urgent letters should be sent by APS express service or by international couriers such as DHL and UPS. For domestic deliveries Aras Kargo, or one of the other domestic couriers, provide a nationwide next-day service.

TELEVISION

There are lots of TV stations broadcasting in Turkish and several of the state-run TRT channels have a few English language programs. Türk Telekom offer cable-TV, which includes BBC World, CNN, NBC and other European channels, or you can sign-up for the cable network Digiturk, which has many more foreign entertainment, news and sport channels.

Education,Language&Crime

It is worth trying to learn some simple Turkish phrases so you can communicate with local people

Crime

Turkey is very safe with crime rates far lower than most European countries, including the UK. You should be wary of pick-pockets in major cities and tourist resorts, but street crime is actually very rare. Property crime is also unusual, but you should take the necessary precautions to secure your apartment or villa, particularly if it is empty for long periods of time. Get to know your neighbours and ask them to keep an eye on things for you. If you are the victim of any kind of crime report the incident immediately to the police, who will file a report. You will need a copy of this for any subsequent insurance claim.

EDUCATION

Turkey's young and rapidly growing population puts immense pressure on the country's education system. Turkish children must complete eight years of compulsory education, but the standard of schooling is often low due to large classes, poor facilities and chronic under-funding. The state school system is divided into nursery, primary and secondary schools, with students normally attending classes either in the morning or the afternoon. Foreign nationals living in Turkey are entitled to send their children to Turkish state schools, although many choose instead to send them to private or international schools. These generally have much better facilities but are only found in the larger cities, such as Istanbul, Ankara, Izmir and Antalya.

LANGUAGE

English is widely spoken in the resorts, particularly by Turks involved in real estate and tourism. Elsewhere, far fewer people speak a foreign language, so it is a good idea to try learning some Turkish. Learning any foreign language requires hard work and perseverance, and Turkish is no different. As a Ural-Altaic language, with little in common with English or Latin-based languages, such as French or Italian, you will have to learn the grammar and vocabulary from scratch. On the plus side, Turkish is a phonetic language, so once you have learnt the basic sounds for each of the letters you should be able to pronounce words correctly. There are various self-study books to help you teach

yourself Turkish, or you may prefer to enroll in a class at a language school in Turkey (see the Directory). There may even be Turkish evening classes near where you live in the UK.

One of the best ways of learning any language though, is getting out and trying to talk to people. Learn a few simple phrases to practice at the market or in your local shop. No matter how bad you are, the fact that you are making an effort will really impress people. Another good way to learn is to swap lessons with someone wanting to learn English.

Health&Healthcare

Should you fall ill in Turkey, private hospitals and clinics offer very high standards of treatment and care

In Turkey there are state-run hospitals (*Devlet Hastaneleri*); hospitals that are funded by the equivalent of National Insurance (*SSK Hastaneleri*) and private clinics and hospitals (*Özel Hastaneler*). There are also teaching hospitals attached to universities in the main cities. State hospitals vary greatly, but are often poorly funded, crowded and may not have up-to-date equipment. Many staff will not speak English. Having said that, in an emergency you will probably receive completely satisfactory treatment. Social Security Hospitals are only open to those who pay into the Turkish social security system. The teaching hospitals attached to some universities, such as Ege University in Izmir or Akdeniz University in Antalya, have a good reputation.

Standards of care are also high in the private sector and there are private hospitals and clinics in the main cities and resorts. An increasing number of "medical tourists" are actually travelling from Europe to take advantage of the excellent medical treatment and lower costs in Turkey. The cost of treatment is far lower than in the UK, but you should check with your insurance company before starting any treatment (see below).

In small towns and rural areas government clinics (*Poliklinik*) are often the only providers of heathcare. Standards vary greatly, but are normally adequate for minor injuries and ailments. Turkish doctors specialise in a particular area of medicine and English-speaking practitioners can be found in most cities and resorts. Fees are reasonable with a check-up costing £30-£50, which includes a follow-up appointment after 10 days.

HEALTH INSURANCE

Private health insurance for people living abroad is available from companies such as BUPA. Like normal health insurance, international policies have varying levels of cover, with the option of repatriation to the UK if you should fall seriously ill. Treatment can be undertaken in any recognised hospital or clinic, but check with your insurer that your policy covers the proposed treatment before you get underway.

Medical insurance schemes are also available from Turkish companies, such as Axa Oyak (see the Directory). If you travel to Turkey to look for property don't forget to buy travel insurance with sufficient medical cover.

VACCINATIONS

No special vaccinations are required before you travel to Turkey, although it is a good idea to check that your tetanus and typhoid cover is up-to-date and have a hepatitis A jab. Malaria has made an appearance in recent years in the far south east of the country, but this is a long way from the areas that you are likely to buy property.

FOR MEDICAL EMERGENCIES DIAL 122

Note: Turkey does not have a well developed ambulance system, so a taxi is often the fastest way of getting to hospital

Food&Shopping

One of the delights of being in Turkey is the fresh seasonal produce available in shops and markets

Fruit and vegetables are generally much fresher and tastier than in the UK. Many come and go with the seasons, although things like tomatoes, peppers, lettuce, apples and imported bananas are available year-round. The last few years have seen the arrival of kiwis and avocados, which are now grown in the country. The Turkish staple is bread, although rice and potatoes are also widely eaten.

DINING OUT

There is an excellent choice of places to eat in Turkish cities and resorts these days. Istanbul has lots of world-class restaurants, offering everything from Asian fusion to traditional Ottoman cuisine. Restaurants serving European food, not always terribly well, alongside Turkish dishes are common in the holiday resorts. More traditional options include grills, called *ocak başı*, where kebabs, chops and steaks are cooked on coals. Fish restaurants are very popular, and you normally select your dinner from a glass-fronted refrigerator. In both types of restaurant you can choose from a huge selection of traditional Turkish starters, known as *meze*. For a quick snack, buffets serving doner kebabs are on most street corners, or the restaurants serving stews, casseroles and soups from stainless steel steam-trays are another good lunch option.

Food retailing has developed rapidly in Turkey in the last decade with large supermarket chains now present in all towns and resorts. As well as domestically produced goods - many of which are exported to Europe - supermarkets also stock imported foods, with some familiar British brands available in the larger coastal resorts. The main supermarket chains include Migros, Tansaş and Carrefour, while Tesco has recently entered the Turkish market through its purchase of Turkish superstore chain Kipa. Modern shopping malls are a convenient place to shop in cities like Istanbul, Antalya and Izmir, as you can find supermarkets, clothes shops, bookstores and DIY outlets all under one, air-conditioned roof. Small shops, known as *bakkal*, are found on most street corners. They usually stock fresh bread, milk, tinned foods, cigarettes and newspapers. For fruit and vegetables you need to visit the local greengrocer (*manav*). Many local shops do not accept credit cards and prices are a bit higher than in supermarkets.

The best places to buy fresh produce and experience local culture are the weekly markets (*pazar*). These have dozens of stalls selling fresh, seasonal fruit and vegetables, cheeses, meat, fish, olives and nuts. Fun and interesting places to shop, markets are also the most economical place to buy groceries. Shopping in local shops and markets is a good way to practice your Turkish. Most shopkeepers won't speak any English, so a few Turkish words and numbers are very useful.

Furniture

There's a wide choice of furniture and electrical equipment at reasonable prices but importing is an option too

REMOVAL COMPANIES

If you are shipping furniture to Turkey use an established international removal company and member of the British Association of Removers (see the Directory). Removal firms charge according to the location and the volume of goods to be moved, and will send a surveyor to your home to give you a quote. As a rough guide, the cost of moving furniture from a two bedroom flat to one of the coastal resort is £3,000-£6,000.

CUSTOMS

Anything to do with Turkish customs is notoriously bureaucratic, so you may want to employ a shipping agent to handle the importation process. You can import furniture and household items into Turkey without paying duty with a valid residence permit. Classed as a "temporary importation", you will need a letter of guarantee from a Turkish bank to leave as a deposit for the unpaid duty. The deposit is returned to you if you leave the country with the furniture, or if you stay more than five years. There are strict rules governing the importation of cars, see page 65. For further information on customs regulations contact the Turkish Embassy, Tel 0207 2456318

ELECTRICAL APPLIANCES

White goods and electrical appliances are manufactured in Turkey - and exported to Europe-by companies such as Beko and Arçelik. These Turkish brands are high-quality and much cheaper than imported goods. There are showrooms in most large towns and whatever you buy can be delivered and fitted for a small extra charge.

FURNISHINGS

Good quality furniture and fitted kitchens are available from several nationwide chains, such as Kelebek (see the Directory). You can visit one of their showrooms or look at their range online first. IKEA have opened in Istanbul and Izmir, with a new store scheduled to open in Antalya in 2008. Most towns also have local furniture and kitchen showrooms. Whatever you want, your estate agent will point you in the right direction and purchases can normally be delivered within days.

Higher quality bespoke furniture is available in the larger resorts and cities. The Çukurcuma area of Istanbul is particularly famous for its antique shops, but you can also find real and reproduction antiques in most of the resorts. Brassware is common and carpets and kilims are a local speciality which can add lots of character. Carpet shops also have inexpensive accessories like saddle bags, cushion covers and throws.

If you are shipping furniture to Turkey use an established international removal company

71

Renting Your Property

The rental market is buoyant in the cities but rental income can't be relied on to finance a property in the resorts

At A Glance
Renting Your Property

✓ Stick to the main cities for buy-to-let purchases
✓ Choose the right kind of property for the location
✓ Holiday rental season is 12-14 weeks in the coastal resorts
✓ Employ a property management company

Many people buying in Turkey want to rent their property out for part of the year. The promise of rental returns on top of strong capital growth has attracted many investors; while those buying primarily for their own use often decide that a few weeks rental can cover the cost of maintaining their property. The Turkish holiday rental market certainly has potential. Over one million British holidaymakers visit Turkey each year, and the government has ambitious plans to nearly double the number of visitors to 30 million each year by 2010. The proportion of visitors choosing to book flights and accommodation, often a villa or apartment, themselves rather than a package holiday, is also growing rapidly too. Increasing flight options and the eventual arrival of low-cost carriers into the coastal airports will encourage this trend, and the rental market as a whole.

In the larger cities like Istanbul, Izmir and Antalya the rental market is year-round and demand is high due to rapidly growing urban populations and an overall shortage of housing. Annual rental yields of 6%-9%, on top of rapidly increasing values, are attracting a growing number of international buy-to-let landlords. The demand for high-quality, well-located property for seasonal and long-term lets is also growing in some of the largest resorts, like Alanya, as the local economies grow.

By contrast, the holiday rental market is far less developed. The on-going building boom has also created a huge pool of rental units with an over-supply in most of the resorts. This makes it very important to choose the right kind of property if

Apartment complexes, like this one in Ovacık, are popular with families

A Buyer's Tale
Rental Fairway

Silvan Ledwell is convinced that the two villas he has bought in the Turkish golfing mecca of Belek will be anything but a handicap for him.

"This is a pension plan for us," says Silvan, a project manager from just outside Colchester in Essex. "We are hoping within a short period of time to rent them out, and in the long term we are looking for a capital return on our investment."

So confident was he of his investment, that he paid for the villas in full once contracts had been signed – and received an attractive discount on the £122,646 price for each of them for doing so.

His search for an investment property began during a golfing holiday in Belek with his wife, Debbi, an accountant. "We did not want to buy in a commercialised resort like Marmaris," says Silvan.

They toured the estate agents looking for detached villas, which were often too large. Having had difficulties renting out their five-bedroom villa in Spain, they wanted a smaller property this time.

Eventually, they decided to buy off plan two semi-detached three-bedroom villas with shared pool, situated opposite the Nick Faldo golf course and within a five-minute drive of several others.

"We thought the properties in Belek were reasonably priced

"The properties are stunning, the prices competitive and the golf is fantastic"

plus you have a resort where you can play golf and be skiing in the mountains close by. We liked the golf but it was the rental potential that was more important for us," says Silvan, who expects to earn €450 (£300) a week from each villa. Service charges will be in the region of €55 (£36) a week.

The couple were impressed with the buying process in Turkey which they found to be far more transparent, although more bureaucratic, than in Spain.

"We saw a lot of documentation and title deeds showing that permissions had been granted and everything properly sanctioned. Everyone spoke English and the

contracts were in English which provided me with a warm feeling all round," says Silvan.

Every week he receives photographs from the estate agency showing how building work is progressing. The villas are due for completion at the end of this year, when they will be asked to select kitchen appliances, tiles and other fittings. Silvan urges potential owners to go to Belek and take a look for themselves. "The properties are really stunning, the prices competitive and the golf is fantastic."

Silvan and Debbie bought from Letsgototurkey, www.letsgototurkey.com

Top-end rental villas must have a private pool

RENTALS AND TAX

Until now, most foreigners renting their properties didn't declare the rental income in Turkey or pay tax. However, the government is tightening up its inspection regime and, partly as a result of complaints from hoteliers losing business, is likely to start taking tax-avoidance by foreign property owners more seriously. Therefore, if you have more than a few informal lets each year, it would be wise to start declaring the income. See page 65 for more information about taxes.

rental is a primary concern. In resorts such as Alanya, Altınkum and Kuşadası, which are popular with families, apartments on complexes are the easiest to rent, because they are cheap and have a range of facilities, much like a hotel. In resorts such as Kalkan or Kaş private villas with pools offer the best rental returns. Also think carefully about the location. Easy access to the beach and facilities is important for families renting an apartment, while those choosing a luxury villa will probably prefer a more secluded spot with a sea view. The furniture in a villa should be carefully chosen to add character and atmosphere. In an apartment, the main concerns are convenience and usability.

The rental season in most of the coastal resorts is from June to the beginning of October, with the summer and autumn half-term holidays, along with July and August, the busiest times. In the larger resorts there is demand from the local population for off-season lets. Winter lets, although at a lower rate, significantly boost annual returns. As part of the area guides in this book we give an assessment of rental potential and typical rates. Wherever your property, successful marketing and management are the key to achieving good returns. Many estate agents and independent firms offer management services, which include cleaning, laundry services, maintenance and welcome baskets. This is very convenient if you are not on-site. The fee for these services is typically 15-20% of the rental income.

UK travel companies specialising in Turkish villa holidays, such as Tapestry and Exclusive Escapes, market suitable properties, paying the owner an annual fee. Typically, owners must sign a contract for at least 3 years and they can reserve several weeks each season for their own use.

Lastly, lots of people choose the DIY approach, advertising their property in a local newspaper, or on one of the many rental websites. Alternatively, they may rely on friends, family and colleagues to spread the word. If you decide to take this route you will need a website and some simple promotional material, including photos of the property and rates. You will also have to organise for someone to see guests in and clean up after they have left, if you are not around yourself.

The Aegean

Ayvalık

The town's Ottoman Greek houses make great renovation projects, or there are bargain villas in the surrounding area

AYVALIK AT A GLANCE
Population: 27,000
Telephone Area Code: 0266
Airport: Izmir (2.5 hours)

PROPERTY LOWDOWN
TYPICAL PRICES
Apartment (2-bed): £35,000
Villa (3-bed): £60,000
Rental Potential: Poor

Advantages:
Atmospheric Turkish town
Many old houses

Disadvantages:
Distance to Izmir airport

AGENTS & DEVELOPERS
Turkish Estates Link
Tel: 020 79872707
www.turkishestateslink.com

On the Aegean coast north of Izmir, Ayvalık is surrounded by countryside carpeted with olive-groves. Famous for olive oil and soap, the town had a large Greek population until 1923. Their memory lives on in the atmospheric old quarter with its impressive houses and churches, which are now mosques. Built by Greek merchants and businessmen at the turn of the last century, some of the grand stone town houses have been renovated in the last 15 years. Many more stand in disrepair.

Across the bay from the town, and reached by a causeway or ferry, is the island of Alibey, where there are more Ottoman-era houses and some excellent fish restaurants. There is a beach at the small resort of Sarımsaklı, 5 km south of Ayvalık town, while in the town centre restaurants overlook the water and there is a busy high-street of shops. There is a marina on the edge of town and a ferry service to the Greek island of Lesbos in the summer.

The Greek houses in the old town and on Alibey make excellent renovation projects. Many are in an advanced state of decay and need virtual re-building, but they are all subject to strict planning controls. Bare in mind that access to some of the houses is difficult as many of the cobbled streets are too narrow for modern vehicles. Instead, building materials are delivered and rubbish taken away by horse-drawn carts.

There are cooperatives and some new villa developments on the island of Alibey, as well as in the suburb of Çamlık and Sarımsaklı. The houses on cooperative developments are often poor quality and need renovating. Prices start from about £35,000 for a small villa on an established cooperative. Expect to pay over £50,000 for a newer house, with some sea-front houses on Alibey fetching over £100,000.

Prices for the old Greek houses vary according to their condition and location. A large newly renovated house with original features typically costs from £55,000-£100,000. Smaller houses or those in need of renovation are available from £25,000; or half that price for a complete wreck. The area is popular with domestic tourists, but there is not a great demand for rental property.

Çeşme

Largely undiscovered by foreigners, Çeşme is deservedly popular with Turkish tourists and second-home owners

Çeşme is a small resort overlooking the Greek island of Chios, 45-minutes from the city of Izmir. Many Turkish families have second-homes in the area and it has become a fashionable holiday spot for young people from Istanbul and Ankara. Despite its domestic appeal, few foreigners visit or buy property.

A Genoese castle stands over the harbour, from where ferries leave for Chios and ports in Italy. Ilıca, 5 km east of the center, has the area's best beach, while nearby Alaçatı, formerly a Greek village, has pretty stone houses and cobbled streets lined with cafes and bars. Alaçatı bay is an internationally renowned windsurfing spot. South of the town, there are more good beaches near the village of Çiftlikköy, which is a pleasant year-round Turkish community. In the opposite direction, Dalyanköy has a harbour surrounded by fish restaurants. There are several marinas in the area, as well as a hot spring and thermal centre. The local dining is varied and the nightlife is excellent in summer. Without a car, access between Çeşme's various resorts is easy with regular minibuses.

Çeşme has a particularly wide choice of property, from cheap coop houses to breathtaking luxury villas. Places in the centre of Çeşme have easy access to facilities, but it is busy in summer. Prices start from £50,000 for a two-bedroom apartment, or from £65,000-£70,000 for a better quality flat, possibly with access to a pool. In Dalyanköy and Çiftlikköy apartments are rare; three-bedroom semi-detached villas are the standard offering. Prices range from £85,000-£105,000, or £120,000-£135,000 for a more luxurious house with pool and sea view.

Ilıca and nearby Paşalimanı are favoured by wealthy Turkish buyers. Expect to pay upwards of £225,000, and often a lot more, for a villa with its own garden and pool. These areas have good access to the beach, and Paşalimanı has great views. Prices in Alaçatı vary widely, with three-bedroom semi-detached villas available from £95,000; newly-built three-bedroom stone houses with communal pool from £130,000; or detached luxury villas from £200,000. Port Alaçatı, an ambitious waterside development based on Port Grimaud in France, is underway near the Alaçatı marina with prices on the current phase from £178,000 for a two-bedroom house. Seasonal lets are common thanks to the area's popularity with Turkish families relocating for the summer.

ÇEŞME AT A GLANCE
Population: 40,000
Telephone Area Code: 0232
Airport: Izmir (1 hour)

PROPERTY LOWDOWN
TYPICAL PRICES
Apartment (2-bed): £68,000
Villa (3-bed): £130,000
Rental Potential: Good

Advantages:
Close to Izmir airport
Good beaches and windsurfing
Excellent selection of property

Disadvantages:
Expensive in parts

AGENTS & DEVELOPERS
Ant Yapı
Tel: +90 216 4560722
www.antyapi.com

Villas in Turkey
Tel: +90 536 4613512
www.villasinturkey.net

77

We at Turkey Expert

assist you at every step of your buying process to make sure that your property purchase runs as smooth as possible.

> Independent advice
on buying property in Turkey

> Friendly and practical guidance
on purchasing your dream home

Being one of the Aegean's most established real estate agents with 20 years of experience and more than 1,000 properties for every budget, our priority is to locate the right investment to meet your specific requirements.

Off-plan, re-sale, apartment, villa, townhouse, commercials,lands, and Professional construction services...

Contact us now:
www.turkeyexpert.co.uk

Kuşadası

The town has grown rapidly into a major holiday resort and property hot spot with good facilities and services

Kuşadası has grown into a large resort town popular with British, Irish and domestic holidaymakers. The recently re-developed cruise ship terminal is Turkey's largest, with thousands of passengers disembarking to visit the nearby archaeological site of Ephesus, one of the country's most important tourist attractions, and the Virgin Mary's chapel. There are many other sights nearby, and the Dilek National Park, 30 km south, has beaches and forest walks. Plans for two golf courses have been approved, with work expected to commence late in 2007. A convention centre is also under construction. The town centre has a good selection of shops and services. There is a large yacht marina and beaches to the north and south of the center. Kadınlar Denizi (Ladies' Beach), to the south, is the area's best-known beach.

Kuşadası has experienced explosive growth in recent years. Much of the building is for Turkish buyers but there are over 3,500 foreign property owners too. Over-development has spoilt some parts of the town, however, local planning regulations have recently been changed to try and address the problem. On the plus side, there is a wide choice of property, though with such a large supply it is important to buy on high-quality developments in the best locations.

Apartments predominate in the centre but there are also some older villas. Prices start from £30,000 for a basic two-bedroom apartment, or from £40,000 on a decent development near the marina. The Ladies' Beach area is more expensive, particularly if you want a sea view. Near the beach expect to pay £40,000-£55,000 for a new two-bedroom apartment, or from £68,000 for a three-bedroom villa on a complex with pool.

South of the town, Long Beach and Davutlar have beaches backed by orchards and some huge cooperative developments. It is a much quieter area, although minibuses into Kuşadası run every few minutes during the season. Prices are lower than in town, with a new-build villa with shared pool costing from £50,000. Older houses are available from just £25,000 but the quality will be poor. The village of Soğucak, 6 km south of town, is surrounded by pretty countryside and has a selection of villas and land.

KUŞADASI AT A GLANCE
Population: 60,000
Telephone Area Code: 0256
Airport: Izmir (45 mins)

PROPERTY LOWDOWN
TYPICAL PRICES
Apartment (2-bed): £45,000
Villa (3-bed): £75,000
Rental Potential: Poor

Advantages:
Close to Izmir airport
Year-round facilities
Good beaches and sights

Disadvantages:
Unsightly development in parts

AGENTS & DEVELOPERS
Capital Developments
Tel: +90 256 6133708
www.capitaldevelopments.net

Turkey Expert
Tel: +90 256 6131770
www.turkeyexpert.co.uk

Property of Turkey
Tel: +90 5334232981
www.propertyofturkey.com

Expert View
Kuşadası

What sets Kuşadası apart from the other Turkish resorts?

Kuşadası is within easy reach of Izmir airport, which is open throughout the year for charter flights. It has hundreds of shops and restaurants - most of which don't close down in winter. Kuşadası also has the longest sandy beach (13 miles) on the Aegean Coast. There are three water parks, an excellent marina and Turkey's largest cruise ship harbour with up to eight ships visiting each day. The historical sites of Ephesus and the Temple of Artemis (one of the Seven Wonders of the World) are 15 minutes from town. There are also several hospitals including an excellent private hospital. All this means that Kuşadası is not only a place to retire or for holidays, but the most cosmopolitan town on the Aegean coast.

Is Kuşadası property a good investment?

Buying a property in Kuşadası is an excellent investment. You can get a very high standard property from as little as £520 per m2. Local prices have tripled since 2002, and the minimum increase you can expect in the next three years is 15% per annum.

Which areas of Kuşadası would you recommend to property buyers, and why?

Kuşadası is a diverse area

"The minimum price increase you can expect is 15% per annum"

which offers something to suit most buyers. Ladies Beach has lots of restaurants, bars and entertainment, as well as a good sandy beach, all just 3 km from the centre of the town. In Yavansu, 3.5 km

from the centre, you get a lot of property for your money - a four-bed semi-detached villa costs just £49,000, for example. Long Beach is further from town and is a quiet area with a long sandy beach, a good choice of local restaurants and a water park. It is ideal for families. Soğucak offers high profile properties in a more rural setting and often with amazing sea views.

Which areas are the best for rental?

Property in all parts of Kuşadası is rentable but the closer you are to the centre the higher your chances of finding a long-term tenant. Long-term rental rates are lower than seasonal or holiday lets but a long-term tenant pays monthly service charges and there are no void periods.

Do you have any general advice for people buying in Turkey?

If you are buying primarily for investment reasons you should consider buying off-plan. However, not all developments will turn out to be a good investment. Seek professional help from an established real estate company and do not hesitate to consult a solicitor for further assistance.

Christine Altinay is the director of Turkey Expert, www.turkeyexpert.co.uk

A Buyer's Tale
Newly Converted

Semi-retirement cannot come quick enough for Barrie Reckless. He and his wife Jacqueline have bought a penthouse duplex apartment in Altınkum. The couple from South Yorkshire moved into the duplex apartment last April. "It is like a dream come true," says managing director Barrie, who has recently sold two of his three businesses. "What we have bought is absolutely fantastic."

As well as a double bathroom and two Jacuzzi baths, the four-bedroom duplex has air-conditioning, a large kitchen, barbecue on the balcony and views towards the mountains on one side and the sea , 900 metres away, on the other. They paid £65,000 for the property and a share in the freehold, £800 for the property tax and transaction costs, £400 utility connection charges and a 3% estate agency fee. Barry says furniture is much cheaper than at home and the cost of living extremely low by comparison. Their dream, however, was not always on the cards. Having been persuaded to visit Turkey by his sales director, whose brother lived in Turkey, Barrie was not immediately impressed.

"On a scale of one to five, I'd have given the properties we saw minus five," says Barrie. "I had never been to Turkey, I'd always been to Greece and it was not until the last night

"I didn't know anything about buying property but it was no hassle"

of my trip that I looked in the estate agent's window and saw this property, which had previously caught my eye." He viewed it the very next day and was so impressed with the high standard of finishing that he paid a holding fee. He also had a long talk with the estate agent, who inspired confidence. "I didn't know anything about buying property in Turkey but it was no hassle whatsoever," he admits.

He says the estate agent dealt with every aspect of the buying process right up to and including legal representation and buying furniture. "I was really happy with the way they handled things. Everything has gone extremely smoothly, even though the Turkish government moves very slowly with all the checks." He returned to Turkey four times whilst the apartment was being finished just to keep an eye on things. After paying a deposit, he made two further instalments, with the final £2,000 and estate agency fees paid on completion.

He believes the time is right to buy property in Turkey as prices are low, although rising. "It is a good time for investment," says Barrie. "Plus interest rates are high so we are getting 20% on money in the bank."

Barrie and Jacqueline bought from Turkish Connextions, www.turkishconnextions.co.uk

tc turkish connextions

Beautiful homes in the sun

"Visit the country with so much to offer; sun, sea, sandy beaches, and a country offering a vast amount of historical wealth."

NEW DEVELOPMENT:

Turquoise Bay Complex
Tuzla / Bodrum

A selection of 2 Bed apartments
from £53,600

3 Bed Duplex's with insuite Bathrooms
from £95,600

4 minutes from the Vita Park Golf Club

NEW FOR 2007

Mimosa Altinkum

2 bed Apartments, some with
separate kitchen prices from £35,000

Duplex's 3 beds prices from £65,000

Excellent location 500 metres
from sea front

www.turkishconnextions.co.uk
Tel: 01772 735151

Altınkum

With its sandy beaches and cheap property, Altınkum is one of the most popular places for British buyers

The resort of Altınkum has a series of sandy beaches and is particularly popular with British holidaymakers. The town has over 8,000 foreign property owners, mostly British, and a rapidly growing expatriate community. The seafront is lined with restaurants and bars, and in summer there are water sports and leisure activities on the beach, which is ideal for children. Didyma's famous Temple of Apollo is in the town and ancient Greek Miletus and Priene are close by. A 625-berth marina is due for completion in 2009.

Altınkum is a 90-minute drive from Bodrum airport. There is a new public hospital, with larger private hospitals in Bodrum and Kuşadası. Shopping facilities are good with several large supermarkets and a weekly market for fresh produce.

The town has a wide choice of property with some of the lowest prices on the Turkish coast. Apartments are most common with prices starting from £25,000 for a basic two-bedroom flat, located a long way from the beach. However, well-constructed two-bedroom apartments, 5-10 minutes walk from the main beach, cost £40,000-£50,000; or £50,000-£75,000 for a three- or four-bedroom duplex. Apartments at this price level are a much better investment than cheaper property, and complexes should have a decent size pool and other facilities.

Away from the center there are more villa developments, with areas like Çamlık and Aytepe offering quieter surroundings a short minibus ride from the main beach and shopping. Detached three-bedroom villas cost £90,000-£120,000; large four-bedroom villas with garden £120,000-£150,000.

The infrastructure has struggled to keep pace with development in parts of Altınkum. Some access roads are unsurfaced and become muddy or even impassable during the winter. There are drainage problems in low-lying areas. The on-going building boom has created a large supply property, so choosing somewhere with good facilities, located near the beach, is important.

The small resort of Akbük, 10 km south of Altınkum, is popular with buyers wanting more peaceful surroundings, though facilities are limited, particularly in winter when many businesses close down and most houses are empty. The area has resale, new and off-plan villas, which are excellent value for money. Three-bedroom villas cost £55,000-£85,000 and land with building permission is also available.

ALTINKUM AT A GLANCE
Population: 30,000
Telephone Area Code: 0256
Airport: Bodrum (1.5 hours)

PROPERTY LOWDOWN
TYPICAL PRICES
Apartment (2-bed): £50,000
Villa (3-bed): £90,000
Rental Potential: Fair

Advantages:
Good beaches
Cheap property

Disadvantages:
Built-up and crowded in summer
Poor infrastructure in some areas

AGENTS & DEVELOPERS
Altınkum Homes
Tel: 029 20419058
www.altinkumhomes.com

Solmet
Tel: 0207 6241782
www.solmet.co.uk

Turkish Connextions
Tel: 01772 735151
www.turkishconnextions.co.uk

Turkish Premier Homes
Tel: +90 256 8135856
www.turkishpremierhomes.com

Bodrum

Ancient Halicarnassus is now Turkey's best-known resort, with an airport, marinas and golf courses adding to its appeal

Bodrum is one of Turkey's largest and most cosmopolitan resorts. A fishing and farming community in the shadow of a magnificent crusader castle thirty years ago, the town's history stretches back 2,000 years, to when it was the capital of the ancient kingdom of Caria and home to one of the 'Seven Wonders of the World' – the tomb of Mausolus. More recently, Bodrum was a bohemian retreat for Turkish artists and intellectuals, before developing into a tourist mecca attracting European and domestic holidaymakers, as well as Turkish high-society. Renowned for its plush bars and energetic clubs, the town also boasts excellent restaurants and a museum in the restored Castle of St John.

Local healthcare provisions are very good with several private hospitals. Shopping is also good with a choice of supermarkets and a weekly market. There is a large marina and a new terminal for cruise liners. Two golf courses are nearing completion near the airport, 25 km from the town centre. Beyond the town itself, the Bodrum peninsular is ringed by a series of smaller, quite distinct resorts.

Bodrum is very popular with foreign and Turkish buyers and there is an excellent choice of property. Apartments with views of the castle typically start from £90,000 for two-bedrooms; or from £190,000 for a three-bedroom villa. Elsewhere in Bodrum or nearby Konacık, which is closer to the excellent beach at Bitez, good quality two-bedroom apartments cost £55,000-£85,000.

Large parts of Turgutreis, at the western end of the peninsular, are a military zone and off-limits to foreign buyers. The resort has a new marina and is popular with package holidaymakers, particularly from Britain.

The area around Gümüşlük has become a focus for development. The village is several kilometres inland

BODRUM AT A GLANCE
Population: 40,000
Telephone Area Code: 0252
Airport: Bodrum (25 mins)

PROPERTY LOWDOWN
TYPICAL PRICES
Apartment (2-bed): £70,000
Villa (3-bed): £135,000
Rental Potential: Fair

Advantages:
Plenty of summer flights
Good restaurants and nightlife
Wide choice of property

Disadvantages:
Crowded in the summer
High prices in some areas
Built-up in parts

from a small bay, with a row of excellent fish restaurants and a pretty beach. Property in the village is mostly resale, with some renovated stone cottages and larger villas starting from £110,000. Building near the beach is strictly controlled due to the archaeological remains of ancient Mindos, but there is lots of property along the coast towards Yalıkavak. Prices start from £35,000 for a basic resale apartment with two bedrooms, or from £60,000 for a larger, better quality new-build flat with two-bedrooms and sea views. Old villas are available from £40,000 though the quality of build will be poor; while a new two-bedroom semi-detached villa on a complex with pool starts from £70,000.

Yalıkavak has a wide selection of property from apartments and villa complexes to luxury mansions. The centre is pleasant with a smart marina, shops, restaurants and a waterfront promenade. Similar to Gümüşlük, some property sold as being in "Yalıkavak" may be a long way from the centre. Local prices have risen rapidly and three-bedroom villas now cost from £100,000-£175,000 depending on how close to the sea they are, facilities and quality of build. Prices are similar in the neighbouring resort of Gündoğan, which has a protected beach backed by small hotels, restaurants and villa developments. A new-build four-bedroom villa with a pool and views of the sea typically costs £165,000-£200,000. Larger, more luxurious properties are available in Yalıkavak, Gündoğan and Göltürkbükü, which is favoured by the Turkish jet-set.

A number of large developments are underway in Tuzla, near the airport and golf courses. Prices are low with one-bedroom apartments available off-plan from under £30,000. But golf aside facilities in the area are very limited and Bodrum is a 20-minute drive away. A possible compromise is the town of Güllük, which is close to the golf courses but has some restaurants and shops around a small harbour.

Despite a lot of competition nice properties can achieve relatively good rental returns with holiday lets from £250-£300 per week for a two-bedroom apartment and from £600 for a villa. Long lets at significantly lower rates are also possible in Bodrum town.

AGENTS & DEVELOPERS
Cumberland Properties
Tel: 0207 4358113
www.cumberland-properties.com

Dream Homes Worldwide
Tel: 0800 0193847
www.dreamhomesww.com

Harmony Homes
Tel: +90 252 363 9616
www.harmonyhomesbodrum.com

Seaside Properties
Tel: +90 252 3637191
www.seasidepropertiesturkey.com

The harbour in Gümüşlük

A Buyer's Tale
Blind Date

It was love at first sight when investment banker, Chris Green, and his Turkish wife, Nazan, a teacher, visited Gümüşlük on the Bodrum peninsular. They loved it so much that they decided to buy a two-bedroom duplex on a gated development off-plan there and then. In fact, the purchase was something of a blind date. The couple had taken an inspection flight with another company but they didn't like their properties, so Chris contacted another company, run by a friend of a friend.

"We had a good look round first but we fell in love with Harmony Gardens," says a delighted Chris. "It is in a secluded position only a kilometre from the beach, well served by the local bus and surrounded by mandarin trees."

The Greens viewed a couple of apartments first, but liked the extra space a duplex gave and it had a garden too. Because Chris knew the developer, he signed a contract straight away, without getting it checked over by a solicitor.

"If it had been a developer I

"The developers were flexible and they even changed the payment plan"

didn't know I would have got the contracts checked by a solicitor in the UK but because I knew them, I was happy to sign whilst I was over there," he said. "The whole process was straight forward."

He had done his homework first, however. He checked out the developer's previous sites and spoke to people who had bought from them before. A deposit of £10,000 was paid upfront with the remaining £45,000 due in instalments - £7,000 at the end of this year and the balance on completion in 2008. Service fees will be around £30 a month.

"The developers were flexible with the terms and even changed the payment plan to when I thought I would have funds available," says Chris. "There was no high pressure sales pitch and we

had plenty of time to think about it. Even though my wife speaks Turkish, everyone spoke perfect English and the contracts were in English." The couple intend to spend a couple of weeks there each year and may rent it out through the developer's rental scheme, or resell it in the future. They chose Turkey for its low prices, stable economy and availability of charter flights.

"The yields are there but you have to be careful about over-supply of property in certain areas," warns Chris. "You can pick up a two-bedroom place for £17,000 but there are a lot of cowboy developers out there."

Chris and Nazan bought from Harmony Homes, www. harmonyhomesbodrum.com

West Mediterranean

Marmaris

One of Turkey's largest resorts, Marmaris has beaches, entertainment, shopping and a good choice of property

MARMARIS AT A GLANCE
Population: 58,000
Telephone Area Code: 0252
Airport: Dalaman (90 minutes)

PROPERTY LOWDOWN
TYPICAL PRICES
Apartment (2-bed): £70,000
Villa (3-bed): £165,000
Rental Potential: Fair

Advantages:
Beautiful surroundings
Good entertainment and leisure facilities
Excellent healthcare and services

Disadvantages:
Large and built up
Relatively high prices

AGENTS & DEVELOPERS
Aegean Estates
Tel: +90 252 4554303
www.aegeanestates.com

Marmaris sits on a stunning bay enclosed by pine-forested mountains. Ottoman sultan Süleyman the Magnificent built the town's tiny castle before invading Rhodes in 1522, but little else remains of the old fishing village of yesteryear. Modern Marmaris is a large town and one of Turkey's main resorts, receiving over a million visitors each year. It boasts excellent services, entertainment and shopping, as well as several marinas, including the 750-berth Netsel Marina. The town is surrounded by beautiful countryside with plenty of excursion options. The beaches in town aren't good, but the nearby suburb of Içmeler (see picture) has a long sandy beach with water sports. Içmeler's promenade is backed by hotels, behind which are touristy shops, restaurants, villas and small apartment buildings. The area is neat with carefully kept communal gardens and a well-developed infrastructure.

Enclosed by steep mountains, there is very little new land available for development in Marmaris. The town centre is dominated by re-sale apartments, mostly over 5 years old. Close to the main concentration of restaurants, shopping and nightlife, two-bedroom apartments start from £50,000, though the setting is urban and properties rarely have views.

The suburb of Armutalan is popular with foreign and Turkish buyers and counts former Turkish president, Kenan Evren, as one of its residents. The area has a mix of hotels, villas and apartment complexes, with prices for a new two-bedroom apartment from £50,000-over £75,000; or three-bedroom apartments from £75,000-£125,000. Semi-detached villas cost £120,000-£150,000; while detached villas with pools are over £200,000. You can also find cheaper re-sale property.

The suburb of Beldibi, 3 km from the centre, is more Turkish with no tourist infrastructure. There are frequent minibuses into the centre and some properties have views. Prices are similar to Armutalan.

Prices in Içmeler are significantly higher. New two-bedroom apartments cost £90,000-£120,000; £150,000-over £200,000 for a three-bedroom semi-detached villa or over £300,000 for a spacious three-bedroom house with a pool.

Datça

Despite low prices and pretty scenery, the town's isolation means it is ignored by many tourists and property buyers

Sitting on the scenic Reşadiye Peninsular, Datça is a small coastal town built around a pretty harbour. Bad road access from Marmaris, 75 km east, gave it a feeling of isolation and slowed development until fairly recently. The road has now been improved but the distance from Dalaman airport, with transfer times of 2.5 hours, puts many would-be foreign tourists and property buyers off. By contrast, the area is a popular holiday spot for Turkish families, many of whom own second homes in the area. Indeed, the local population quadruples in summer, to about 45,000.

Datça's harbour is a popular port-of-call for yachts, with the tiny, picturesque Greek island of Simi a short cruise off-shore. Several local beaches have been given the coveted Blue Flag award. Beyond the town, the scenery is unspoilt with almond orchards and olive groves descending to quiet coves. The site of the ancient city of Knidos, famous in antiquity for its statue of Aphrodite, sits at the very tip of the Reşadiye peninsular and is a popular day-trip.

There is a car-ferry several times a week from Bodrum in summer. Local shops stock all the essentials and there is a large supermarket.

Most of the area's older properties have been built for the Turkish market and generally need renovating, though prices are very low. In the last couple of years much higher quality apartments and villas have also been built.

Prices in Datça remain significantly lower than Marmaris or Bodrum, with new semi-detached three-bedroom villas with garden and shared pool available from £80,000-£90,000. New two-bedroom apartments typically sell for £40,000-£55,000. Basic re-sale apartments are available from £35,000 and houses from £50,000 or less. Largely ignored by European holidaymakers, rental potential is poor at present.

DATÇA AT A GLANCE
Population: 8,800
Telephone Area Code: 0252
Airport: Dalaman (2.5 hours)

PROPERTY LOWDOWN
TYPICAL PRICES
Apartment (2-bed): £48,000
Villa (3-bed): £85,000
Rental Potential: Poor

Advantages:
Unspoilt surroundings
Smaller, quieter resort
Cheap property

Disadvantages:
Distance from the airport

AGENTS & DEVELOPERS
Aegean Estates
Tel: +90 252 4554303
www.aegeanestates.com

Dalyan

A low-key riverside resort set in beautiful countryside with interesting attractions and a good selection of villas

Dalyan is a small resort of family-run guesthouses, hotels and villas sitting beside a lazy river that winds its way between Lake Köyceğiz and the sea. Magnificent rock-cut tombs, dramatically illuminated at night, overlook the town; while the extensive ruins of the ancient city of Kaunos are a short walk from the centre. Other local attractions include thermal mud baths and the 13 km-long beach at Iztuzu, which is protected as a nesting site for the endangered loggerhead sea turtle. Indeed, the whole area is a haven for wildlife and birds.

The town has a good choice of shops, restaurants and even a small supermarket. The local nightlife is low-key compared to the larger resorts. Health facilities are limited to several doctors and a small clinic, with a state hospital and other services in the district centre of Ortaca, 12 km away. Dalaman airport is a 25-minute drive.

Local planning regulations have limited development to villas and small apartment complexes. Property prices are much higher than in neighbouring Dalaman. Most new properties are in the residential areas of Gülpınar, Maraş, Arık Başı and Marmarlı, which have grown up on farmland, 10-20 minutes walk from the centre. Plot sizes are generally 500m2, which may accommodate several small villas or more apartments depending on the planning restrictions. A fairly basic semi-detached house costs £80,000-£90,000; a three-bedroom villa with pool from £125,000. Larger villas with more spacious gardens cost £130,000-over £200,000. The choice of apartments is more limited though there are a number of new developments on the edge of town. A new two-bedroom apartment with communal pool costs £55,000-£65,000; or £60,000-£70,000 for a three-bedroom. Cheaper resale houses and apartments, often on small complexes with communal gardens and pool, are also available, but these are generally fairly small and may need refurbishing. Plots of land, typically 500m2, are available in all the areas mentioned above for £50,000-£60,000. It is possible to earn a reasonable return from private holiday lets but successful marketing is required.

DALYAN AT A GLANCE
Population: 4,000
Telephone Area Code: 0252
Airport: Dalaman (25 mins)

PROPERTY LOWDOWN
TYPICAL PRICES
Apartment (2-bed): £60,000
Villa (3-bed): £135,000
Rental Potential: Fair

Advantages:
Pretty surroundings
Lots of local sights and activities
Close to Dalaman airport

Disadvantages:
Limited entertainment
Relatively high property prices

AGENTS & DEVELOPERS
Lycia Properties
Tel: 01282 446035
www.propertyinturkey.com

Niobe Properties
Tel: +90 252 284 3946
www.niobeproperty.com

Delta Real Estate
Tel: +90 252 284 3281
www.dalyandelta.com

A Buyer's Tale
Part Exchange

Dalyan has well and truly cast its magic on teacher Rosemary Demaine from Blackburn. She has just bought her second villa there, part-exchanging the first for a larger property. Rosemary first visited the area two years ago after reading a book about the fight to protect the local turtle beach from hotel development. Passionate about conservation, she says she felt instantly at home there. "Having worked in the travel industry I have travelled the world but have never felt as comfortable, relaxed or safe as I did there," she says.

After researching on the internet, she returned a few months later to buy a villa, though she quickly decided she wanted a property with more land. A passionate gardener, Rosemary says she wanted a bigger garden, in which to grow vegetables, and a larger swimming pool. She found a 550 m2 plot with planning permission on the village outskirts through a local developer, and working closely with their architect and builder, she set about designing a three-bedroom

"Rosemary did not want the usual open-plan design downstairs"

villa for herself.

Rosemary did not want the usual Turkish open-plan design downstairs, preferring to create a separate lounge with central fireplace, which she says will be warmer in the winter. There is also a large kitchen/ diner, lounge, utility room and bathroom with shower downstairs, and three bedrooms and a bathroom with bath and shower upstairs, plus swimming pool and driveway with a car-port. Rosemary describes the villa as "very attractive" with white marble steps up to the front door.

She chose the developer because they offered a one-stop service, which included furnishing the villa and landscaping the garden. They even planted flowers and installed an automatic

sprinkler system.

"Everything was taken care of. It came fully furnished and was ready to move in – there was even food in the fridge," says Rosemary, who moved in last May. "It was so easy to do, totally stress free."

Having sold her previous property in part-exchange for the new villa, she paid a £10,000 deposit, followed by £15,000 and a final payment of £25,000 on completion. She pays £75 a month for pool and garden maintenance. Rosemary plans to spend around 10 weeks a year there with her nine-year-old daughter, Rebecca. The rest of the time she will rent it out to family and friends.

Rosemary bought from Niobe Properties, www.niobeproperty.com

Lycia
properties in
Turkey

Sarigerme the new Turkish golf resort

- 15 min from Dalaman International Airport
- Excellent investment opportunity
- Completion of first golf course planned for 2009
- Beautiful sandy beaches
- Exclusive sea view apartments and Villas
- Prices inclusive of all costs (no hidden extras)
- Great off plan discounts
- Full after sales support
- Mortgages now available

For more information on our new projects
in Sarigerme, Fethiye and Dalyan please contact

www.propertyinturkey.com

email: info@propertyinturkey.com • tel: UK 01282 44 6035 • tel: Turkey +90 252 612 9128

Curbanoglu
DESIGN & CONSTRUCTION

Unique Location
Breath-taking Property

Akkaya, Dalaman
15 mins from Dalaman international airport
20 mins from new golf course & beaches

Superb investment, exclusive living
Villas from £79,000
Apartments from £55,000

Buy direct from a trusted developer with over 1,600 completed homes
Call now for more information about this unique opportunity:
Tel: 0845 355 5625   www.curbanoglu.co.uk

Dalaman&Sarıgerme

Beautiful countryside, an airport and a golf course underway are encouraging lots of interest from buyers and investors

An agricultural area growing citrus fruit, vegetables and cotton, Dalaman was put on the tourist map by its international airport, which was expanded with the addition of a large new international terminal last year. Hundreds of thousands of tourists pass through each season on their way to the coastal resorts, although comparatively few stay. However, a government-led plan to promote tourism in the area includes a new golf course, marina, spa centre, hotels and residential areas.

Dalaman itself is a work-a-day market town spread across a flat plain. Although not very picturesque, it offers a slice of real Turkish life. The municipality has been improving the centre and the shops and restaurants are becoming increasingly geared to providing for the area's tourist population.

The surrounding mountains are green and unspoilt. There is white water rafting on the Dalaman River and a long beach at Sarıgerme, 12 km south of the town. Several large hotel complexes sit on the Blue Flag-awarded shoreline, with a new golf course due for completion at the end of 2008.

The government-led development plans for the area have caused intense interest from buyers and investors. The resulting increases in land and property values have been dramatic, even by Turkish standards. These increases have slowed in the last year but prices are still well below other resorts.

There is a wide choice of new and off-plan property in and around the town, but the quality of construction is variable so opt for a company that has a track record of well-built developments. A three-bedroom villa with pool currently costs £75,000-£95,000. A two-bedroom apartment on a complex with communal facilities costs £40,000-£55,000 - or cheaper if you buy off-plan. There are also cheaper re-sale houses and apartments in the area, though they generally need renovating.

Sarıgerme is more expensive due to its proximity to the beach and golf course, with a three-bedroom villa with pool costing £100,000-over £120,000. Two-bedroom apartments cost £75,000-£85,000. Many properties have sea views. Plots of land are available with 500m2 costing £55,000-£65,000. A Turkish solicitor should conduct thorough searches as much of the area has building or land-use restrictions.

DALAMAN AT A GLANCE
Population: 17,600
Telephone Area Code: 0252
Airport: Dalaman (5-15 mins)

PROPERTY LOWDOWN
TYPICAL PRICES
Apartment (2-bed): £50,000
Villa (3-bed): £120,000
Rental Potential: Fair

Advantages:
Close to airport
Good beach
Golf course under construction

Disadvantages:
Limited tourist infrastructure
Quiet in winter

AGENTS & DEVELOPERS
Curbanoglu
Tel: 0845 3555625
www.curbanoglu.co.uk

Dalaman Turkish Villas
Tel: +90 252 692 5398
www.dalamanturkishvillas.com

Lycia Properties
Tel: 01282 446035
www.propertyinturkey.com

A Buyer's Tale
Dalaman Dreams

"It was hard to believe that we could have a part of somewhere as beautiful as this," recounts Kathryn Higgins, a manager at NHS Blood & Transfusion. "Even when we saw it for the first time on a cold winter day it looked amazing."

Kathryn and her partner Gerry Stewart, an economics lecturer at Leeds University, arrived in Dalaman in January 2005, having spent months researching into places to buy a holiday home.

"We wanted a place with pretty scenery and an interesting culture," explains Gerry. "We were thinking of Italy, but then we decided on Turkey."

Making a short-term profit was not a concern, although they wanted a sound investment. They booked a viewing trip with a company that had a development in Akkaya, a beautiful rural area overlooking a lake, 20 minutes from Dalaman.

"The location was stunning and we liked the development, but then we were shown some land where we could build our own house," says Kathryn. The couple jumped at the chance of creating their own dream home on a 1,300 m2 plot. They transferred a deposit before returning to the UK, where they searched interior design magazines, emailing pictures to the architect. They also compiled a

"We wanted a place with pretty scenery and an interesting culture"

list of features for the house. "We did a lot of fantasizing, and some of the ideas would have cost too much," laughs Kathryn. "When we returned to see the initial plans we were impressed."

The architect had incorporated most of their ideas and they worked with the design team refining the plans. The house would have a pool and three large bedrooms each with en-suite and large windows and balconies to take advantage of the stunning views. Before returning home to Leeds, they signed a contract so that work could get underway.

"Every month we received a progress report and pictures from the builder," says Kathryn.

They returned to Dalaman to choose fittings and tiles and were pleasantly surprised by the choice available. By the following spring Gerry and Kathryn's dream house was nearing completion. They flew out in May 2006 to spend their first holiday in their new home.

"I was so excited that I couldn't sleep the first night," laughs Gerry.

One year on and they are very happy with their villa, which offers privacy and seclusion, all within a short drive of the town, beach and international airport.

Gerry and Kathryn's villa was built by Curbanoglu, www.curbanoglu.co.uk

Göcek

A yachting centre and upmarket resort surrounded by forested mountains, Göcek has a choice of desirable, top-end property

At the head of a narrow bay surrounded by forested mountains, Göcek is an upmarket resort and a popular summer haunt for some of the country's wealthiest businessmen, politicians and celebrities. An important yachting center with no less than four marinas, the town also attracts an international clientel of cruising and yachting enthusiasts. The pedestrianised promenade is lined with restaurants and bars, with a selection of shops and a small supermarket on the narrow main street. The resort lacks a good public beach, but the Swissotel manages a stretch of sand to the south of the Port Göcek marina. An ambitious development of 130 waterside villas linked to the sea by a network of canals, known as Portville, is underway beside the marina. The coastal highway passes through a new 900-metre road tunnel to the north of Göcek, reducing journey times to Dalaman airport to around 25 minutes.

A lack of flat land and strict local building controls have limited development, with a lot of new property concentrated in the flat area between the town and the ring road. This area is within easy walking distance of the centre, but doesn't have the views offered by properties on the mountainside beyond the coastal highway. There are several new villa and apartment developments on the mountain slopes overlooking the resort, set amongst meadows and woodland.

Property prices in Göcek are high with new villas with no view starting from £135,000-£165,000. Three or four-bedroom detached houses with garden and pool overlooking the town cost £200,000-over £275,000. Several developers have projects that include apartments, with prices starting from £90,000 for two-bedrooms. Plots of land for building are increasingly rare and expensive.

The town has a community of expatriates and Turks working in the yachting industry so long lets are possible.

GÖCEK AT A GLANCE
Population: N/A
Telephone Area Code: 0252
Airport: Dalaman (30 mins)

PROPERTY LOWDOWN
TYPICAL PRICES
Apartment (2-bed): £95,000
Villa (3-bed): £215,000
Rental Potential: Fair

Advantages:
Beautiful location
Strict planning controls
Yachting centre with several marinas

Disadvantages:
High property prices
Limited choice of property

AGENTS & DEVELOPERS
Taurean Properties
Tel: +90 252 6132377
www.taureanproperties.co.uk

Tulip Properties
Tel: +90 252 6136667
www.tulipproperties.com

Fethiye,Çalış,Ovacık&Hisarönü

With good beaches and lots of attractions, plus a wide choice of property, Fethiye remains one of the most popular areas

Stretching around a bay backed by mountains, Fethiye is a bustling town at the heart of one the most popular areas for foreign buyers. As the administrative center for the nearby resorts of Ölüdeniz, Ovacık, Hisarönü and Çalış, the local economy is dominated by tourism, but few tourists stay in the town itself. There is a large harbour and the 400-berth Ece Saray Marina. The town has a pleasant atmosphere with shops and services staying open year-round. Inland from a waterside promenade is a lively bazaar district, known as Paspatur. Other tourist attractions include an amphitheatre and Lycian tombs. There are supermarkets and a huge weekly market, as well as two excellent private hospitals with English-speaking staff.

Fethiye is close to attractions, such as the Saklıkent gorge and ancient Xanthos. The beaches at Ölüdeniz and Çalış are even closer, with regular minibus services to both.

Modern apartments dominate the town and due to a major earthquake in 1957 few old buildings remain. To the west of the center, Karagözler is a residential district where many of the villas and small apartment buildings have superb views over the bay. Prices are high; three-bedroom villas cost £135,000-£200,000. Elsewhere, two-bedroom apartments cost £35,000-over £60,000 depending on the location and quality of build. Cheaper apartments may need extensive renovation. Taşyaka and Deliktaş are popular residential areas to the east of the centre. Taşyaka is almost entirely new apartments typically costing £45,000-£60,000 for two-bedrooms. Building activity is intense, so make sure construction on neighbouring plots isn't going to block your view. The centre of town is a short bus ride away.

The resort of Çalış, 5 km north of Fethiye, has grown-up along a beach lined with hotels and apartments. Popular with British package

FETHİYE AT A GLANCE
Population: 60,000
Telephone Area Code: 0252
Airport: Dalaman (45 mins)

PROPERTY LOWDOWN
TYPICAL PRICES
Apartment (2-bed): £62,000
Villa (3-bed): £120,000
Rental Potential: Fair-Good

Advantages:
Beautiful location with good beaches
Varied tourist attractions
Year-round facilities and services

Disadvantages:
Urban setting and over-developed in parts
High prices in some areas
Resort areas quiet in winter

A Buyer's Tale
Magic Shell

Detective sergeant Steve Appleton fancied building a villa in Turkey himself, and had been researching it for sometime.

"If I could get the right piece of land at the right price I felt I would like to build a project myself," explains Steve, from South Shields in Tyneside. It was at this point he decided to talk to an estate agent in Fethiye, who had sent him details of an unfinished property. In fact, he had had his eye on it for some time. "The villa was one of the first ones I looked at almost a year before. I'd always had it at the back of my mind," says Steve. He went out to Turkey in September 2006 and ended up buying "the concrete shell" at Çalış beach near Fethiye. All he had to do was convince his wife, Julie, an assistant bank manager, that he could find a builder. The estate agent was able to recommend several companies, including one who worked for them.

"Some of his ideas were better than mine so I decided to go with him," laughs Steve, who paid £63,000 for the unfinished three-bedroom detached villa with shared swimming pool.

The shell comprised only the walls and roof; no doors, windows or balconies. With the work underway, Steve visited four times and kept in close touch with the builder, emailing specifications and

"Steve visited four times and kept in close touch with the builder"

drawings of what he wanted and receiving photographs back via the estate agent as work progressed. The job took just 10 weeks: "I signed on 2nd October and it was completed on 20th December," says a delighted Steve, who describes the design as contemporary. The quality of the work was far better than he expected too. As well as doing the electrics, plastering and making the roof watertight, the builder installed solar panels, a bathroom with power shower, travertine tile flooring, double glazing on all the windows, a fully-fitted kitchen with marble work tops, an extra toilet on the ground floor and even a barbecue.

Steve estimates he spent £15,000 on finishing and £5,000 on furnishings and light fittings, making a total of £83,000. The estate agency commission was £1,890. According to Steve, the buying process was "dead easy", as he gave the estate agent power of attorney for the sale and the building work. Their solicitor checked that the necessary building permissions were in place before money was transferred to the vendor. With two teenage children, Steve expects the villa will be used for family holidays three times a year, perhaps four, if he can manage to twist Julie's arm.

Steve and Julie bought from Taurean Properties, www.taureanproperties.co.uk

tourists, the resort now has a large expatriate community. There are restaurants and bars locally, though many close for the winter. Minibuses and water-taxis give easy access to Fethiye, just 10 minutes away. Water sports and excursions are available on the beach in season.

Çalış has expanded rapidly in recent years with development creeping several kilometres inland from the sea. There are off-plan, new and re-sale villas and apartments available. Most new apartments are on complexes with shared facilities and prices vary according to build quality and distance from the beach. Two-bedroom apartments near the sea are £75,000-£85,000, or £48,0000-£65,000 further inland. Three bedroom villas are £90,000-over £130,000. Çalış is a popular holiday resort so rental potential is high. Weekly rates are £250-£300 for a two-bedroom apartment with shared pool; £750-£1,000 for a four-bedroom villa with private pool.

The village of Üzümlü, 19 km from Fethiye, is popular with property buyers looking for peaceful rural surroundings. Three-bedroom detached houses with pool cost £100,000-£155,000. Many houses have sweeping views.

Surrounded by forested mountains, 8 km south of Fethiye, Hisarönü and Ovacık are popular property spots. Strict building controls and a lack of flat land around the picturesque Ölüdeniz lagoon, 4 km south, encouraged development in these neighbouring villages, transforming them into resorts in their own right. They now have hotels, shops, restaurants and bars, though most businesses close for the winter, leaving it very quiet. The scenic setting and easy access to Ölüdeniz have attracted lots of foreign, mainly British, buyers.

Hisarönü and Ovacık have a good selection of new and resale property. A lack of new land and strong demand mean higher prices. Two-bedroom apartments with shared pool cost £65,000-£95,000, with three-bedroom villas with private pool costing £135,000-over £200,000. Prices are highest on the slopes above the main road in Ovacik, from where there are excellent views. Rental potential is good with weekly rates of £800-over £1,000 for a four-bedroom villa with pool.

The nearby village of Kayaköyü, beneath a deserted town abandoned in 1923 by its Greek inhabitants, has some new and older stone houses. Due to the area's historic importance make sure that a Turkish solicitor undertakes thorough searches before buying.

AGENTS & DEVELOPERS

Lycia Properties
Tel: 01282 446035
www.propertyinturkey.com

Taurean Properties
Tel: +90 252 6132377
www.taureanproperties.co.uk

Üzümlü is popular with property buyers looking for peaceful rural surroundings

The beach-front at Çalış

Kalkan
The Jewel of the Mediterranean

Kalkan is a beautiful harbour town that enjoys a fine reputation both within Turkey and abroad and retains its authentic flavour through strict conservation and building codes, as well as the careful protection of 'Green Areas'.

Kalkan, the Jewel of the Mediterranean

Its preserved bougainvillea-covered buildings, sophisticated ambience, dramatic landscape, colourful winding streets, fine dining (including its many famous roof terrace restaurants) and friendly people never fail to charm visitors – and the town has deservedly gained a loyal following. Surrounding Kalkan is the arresting beauty of Lycia with many nearby natural and historical attractions as well as stunning beaches. Due to Kalkan's geography, sweeping views of the Mediterranean are enjoyed from most properties. Combined with the beautiful sunny and warm weather of the area, Kalkan is a most ideal place to live.

The village of Kalkan is an especially beautiful place with superb investment opportunity and excellent rental potential. However, with so much to choose from in terms of location and type, **you want to be sure that you're getting the most suitable,** **best possible property at the best possible price and that the experience will be hassle free.** Mavi Real Estate and Property Services (**www.kalkanproperty.com**) ensures our clients a smooth and easy path to ownership, and we can help beyond the purchase or construction as well. Please browse through our site to see the many properties **we offer and discover how we offer the most complete and comprehensive property buying service in Kalkan** and its environs.

We are a reputable, established estate agency and provide a full, safe, secure and professional service. We sell good quality, sound properties.

We feel very strongly that once you have purchased with us that this is the 'real beginning' of our relationship, not the end.

Kalkan

Overlooking a stunning bay, Kalkan has a great location and one of the best selections of villas on the entire coast

Kalkan is a small but rapidly growing resort tumbling down a mountainside to a harbour filled with yachts. The town itself only has a small stretch of pebbly beach, though the stunning beach at Patara, and the historical sights of the Xanthos valley, are only a short drive away. Kalkan is particularly popular with British tourists, many of who rent villas rather than stay in hotels. The narrow streets leading down to the harbour are lined with restaurants, shops and bars. Buzzing in summer, many businesses close for the winter, when some shops, a supermarket and medical centre remain open. On-going improvements to the coastal highway have cut the journey time from Dalaman airport to around 90 minutes, and the completion of the final stretch into town will reduce this further.

Kalkan has grown explosively in recent years, with major development on the mountainside above the town centre and along the coast. Very little free land remains, although re-zoning of a hillside to the south west of the harbour and a larger area on the edge of town, towards the village of Bezirgan, planned for 2008, will provide new areas for building. Work on a central sewage system is well advanced, replacing septic tanks and tanker collections in many areas. The municipality has privatised rubbish collection, which has improved the service.

In the old town small stone houses occasionally come onto the market. A two-bedroom cottage with courtyard costs £75,000-£110,000, but building and renovation are subject to strict controls. To the west of the town, the quiet residential area of Kalamar Bay has a mix of new and re-sale property, with villas ranging from £155,000-£420,000. Within this price range properties vary from two-bed, semi-detached houses with shared pool, to large detached five-bedroom luxury villas.

Many of Kalkan's apartments are concentrated along the road to Kalamar Bay. Two-bedroom apartments range from £55,000-£95,000. At the top end of this range you should expect a sea view, shared pool and a short walk into the centre. More luxurious newly-built apartments, or duplexes, cost from £95,000-£130,000.

In the opposite direction, Kışla has good views and benefits from cooling sea breezes. The centre is a 20-minute walk away, but the local infrastructure is much improved and there are several beach clubs locally. A three- or four-bedroom villa costs

KALKAN AT A GLANCE
Population: 3,600
Telephone Area Code: 0242
Airport: Dalaman (90 minutes)

PROPERTY LOWDOWN
TYPICAL PRICES
Apartment (2-bed): £80,000
Villa (3-bed): £185,000
Rental Potential: Good

Advantages:
Scenic location
Close to excellent beach and attractions
High-quality property
Good rental potential

Disadvantages:
Limited amenities and quiet off-season
Poor infrastructure in some areas
Distance to airport

AGENTS & DEVELOPERS
Mavi Real Estate
Tel: +90 242 8441220
www.kalkanproperty.com

> There is strong demand for rental villas with a good location and sea views

£165,000-£300,000.

Properties above the town have wonderful open views and may be walking distance from the centre. Prices range from £110,000- over £350,000 depending on the size, quality and location.

In season there is strong demand for rental villas in Kalkan, but choosing a spacious property with a good location and sea views is crucial for achieving successful rental returns. Three-bedroom villas typically rent for £600-700 per week, or from £1,000-over £1,750 per week for larger, more luxurious properties.

Expert View
Kalkan

What is special about Kalkan and how does it compare to other Turkish resorts?
Kalkan has grown a lot in recent years but it still feels like a small seaside town – particularly when compared to the other resorts. There is a real Turkish community along with a well-established group of international property owners. There are a good selection of restaurants, cafes and shops. In addition to great nearby beaches, the area has many archaeological sites. Due to its location on a mountainside, Kalkan is also one of the few Turkish resorts where most new properties still have a sea view.

Is Kalkan property a good investment?
In common with the rest of the coast, local property values sky-rocketed from 2000-2005. Since then the market has slowed, however, I expect annual price increases of 15-20% in the years ahead due to good demand,

"If rental income is important choose a villa"

particularly as the Turkish mortgage market develops. If rental income is important then choose a villa, which are more easily rented than apartments, particularly if they offer spacious accommodation and a sea view.

Which areas of Kalkan would you currently recommend?
Kalamar Bay is still very popular as the local infrastructure is completed and it is easy to get into the town. But for people looking for a bit more space

or to generate a higher rental return, I recommend buying villas above the town. Plots are typically 500-800m2, compared to 300m2 in Kalamar Bay, and the views are fantastic.

Do you have any general advice for people buying in Turkey?
Always deal with professional real estate companies. As a translator, I am often called in to deal with the problems that occur when people buy from waiters or carpet dealers. In order to save yourself 5 or 10%, it isn't worth the risk and it can end up costing you a lot more.
Building quality has improved enormously in recent years, so I recommend buying a newer property. The price may be higher, but you won't have to deal with problems like cracking walls or a leaking swimming pool.

Kemal Safyürek is the owner of Mavi Real Estate, www.kalkanproperty.com

A Buyer's Tale
Banking on Kalkan

Richard and Vicky Wales are banking on a winner with their new five-bedroom villa in Kalkan. The bank managers from Cardiff fell in love with Turkey when Vicky worked in Istanbul for five months and they toured the country.

"We were looking at property but we were playing at it as we hadn't got finances sorted," says Richard, aged 37.

But last year they went on holiday with the intention of buying – and knew Kalkan was where they wanted to be, having visited previously. They contacted a local estate agent, whom they'd met on a previous visit, and were shown around some villas.

The house they ended up buying was one of the first they were shown. "We kept coming back to it," says Richard, adding that it was the large roof top terrace with fantastic views of Kalkan Bay that really sold it to them. "It is the most amazing view at night," he explains.

The couple paid £170,000 for the villa, one of two identical new villas on the plot. One of the five bedrooms is an attic

"You have to be patient as it takes a while for the permissions to come"

room plus there are three bathrooms, including one en-suite, a swimming pool and garden. They have had a second terrace built at the end of the garden.

Daily checks, gardening and maintenance work are carried out by a local company for £1,800 a year. The villa will be used mainly by friends and family

Richard describes the buying process as "nerve wracking" and "taking longer than expected" - around five months in all. However, his sister and her husband buying into the purchase halfway through delayed it by a month.

"You have to be patient as it takes a while for the permissions to come through," says Richard, adding that a

new computerised system should speed things up.

"The process works differently to the UK. You don't have a solicitor controlling the funds, you pay direct to the builder. We were pretty cautious although the estate agent helped us tremendously and gave us complete confidence."

What the couple especially love about Kalkan is its charm, and warm and friendly people. "I have been going to Majorca for 30 years and not one person knows my name," says Richard. "I can walk around Kalkan and bump into 10-15 people who are genuinely pleased to see me. We feel welcome there."

Richard and Vicky Wales bought from Mavi Real Estate, www.kalkanproperty.com

Kaş

A charming town on a beautiful stretch of coast, Kaş has some fantastic property though prices are relatively high

Kaş is a relaxed seaside town overlooking the Greek island of Meis. Formerly a fishing and market centre, tourism now dominates the local economy. Despite this, the town has not been swamped by mass tourism and retains much of its charm. On the site of ancient Antiphellus, Kaş is dotted with archaeological remains, including a small amphitheatre and monumental tombs. The coastline is rocky and beaches are limited to short pebble stretches. The countryside is scattered with more archaeological sites and Kaş is an excellent base for adventure activities. There are plans for a 400-berth marina, which will further promote the area as an up-market holiday venue.

Kaş has an established expatriate community that is swelled in summer by European and Turkish tourists. There are lots of restaurants, several small supermarkets and a weekly market. Medical facilities are limited to a health centre - the nearest hospital is in Fethiye, 90 minutes away.

The 7 km-long Çukurbağ Peninsular is the most desirable part of Kaş and most properties have great sea views. Development is strictly controlled and there are very few building plots left. Three-bedroom villas with shared pool fetch £200,000-£250,000; or £400,000-£600,000 for a four or five-bedroom house with private pool. Two-bedroom apartments cost £80,000-£160,000 depending on the age of the property and its proximity to the sea.

The centre of town has re-sale and new-build apartments. Prices are lower than the peninsular, with a two-bedroom apartment costing £80,000-£130,000; or £120,000-£130,000 for a three-bedroom. At the top of the price ranges you should expect more space and good views from a balcony or terrace.

Above the town, Çerçiler has apartments and villas, many with excellent views and prices are lower. However, many properties don't have title deeds and have been constructed illegally on state land.

Gökseki, to the west of Kaş, has recently been surveyed and title deeds have been issued to about 60% of the properties. A three-bedroom house costs £100,000-£125,000. Rental potential is best on the Çukurbağ Peninsular where villas are in demand.

KAŞ AT A GLANCE
Population: 8,000
Telephone Area Code: 0242
Airport: Dalaman (2 hours)

PROPERTY LOWDOWN
TYPICAL PRICES
Apartment (2-bed): £95,000
Villa (3-bed): £230,000
Rental Potential: Fair-Good

Advantages:
Picturesque location
High-quality property
Good year-round amenities

Disadvantages:
Far from the nearest airport
No good local beaches

AGENTS & DEVELOPERS
Turquaz Emlak
Tel: +90 242 8363620
www.turkuazemlak.com

Tandem Villas
Tel: +90 242 8363287
www.tandemvillas.com

Kemer

A purpose built resort set in stunning scenery, with good beaches and easy access to Antalya

KEMER AT A GLANCE
Population: 17,000
Telephone Area Code: 0242
Airport: Antalya (1 hour)

PROPERTY LOWDOWN
TYPICAL PRICES
Apartment (2-bed): £65,000
Villa (3-bed): £140,000
Rental Potential: Fair

Advantages:
Beautiful surroundings
Close to Antalya airport

Disadvantages:
The town lacks atmosphere.
Limited rental market

AGENTS & DEVELOPERS
Euromedt
Tel: +90 242 2284131
www.euromedt-turkey.com

Kemer is a state planned resort of hotels and apartment complexes 35 km southwest of Antalya. Largely built since the 1980s, the town center is well laid-out but lacks atmosphere. It has good facilities, including a modern marina, shops and several beaches, with a Blue Flag awarded stretch in the town itself. The town's mountainous hinterland, much of it preserved within the Beydağları National Park, is exceptionally beautiful and has some excellent walking. The Lycian Way long distance footpath passes close to the town. Nearby sights include the remains of Phaselis, an important ancient city visited by Alexander the Great. A cable-car to the top of Tahtalı Dağı (2,366 m), the area's highest peak, opened in 2006.

Kemer is popular with Russian tourists, although many of the area's property buyers come from Germany. British buyers are concentrated in the smaller resort of Çamyuva, 5 km south of the town center. Kemer has several supermarkets and private medical facilities. Regular public minibuses link the resort to Antalya, which is under an hour away by car.

Properties in the center are mostly resale apartments costing £50,000-£90,000. Cheaper apartments may need renovation, while more expensive places generally have a communal pool and are close to the sea. Cheaper new and off-plan apartments and villas can be found in Aslanbuçak, 2 km inland from the centre, where a two-bedroom apartment costs £40,000-£55,000. Three-bedroom semi-detached villas cost around £85,000.

Due to local planning regulations restricting building to two-storeys, small apartment complexes and villas are common in Çamyuva. Apartments are generally set in large gardens and have communal facilities and swimming pool. Two-bedroom apartments start from £50,000. A three-bedroom semi-detached villas with pool costs £110,000-£150,000; while larger villas are over £160,000. Land with building permission is also available in the Çamyuva area. The village of Göynük, 10 minutes drive from Kemer, has lower prices and a pleasant community feel.

East Mediterranean

Antalya&Belek

Konyaaltı Beach - the city's summer playground - with the Taurus Mountains in the distance

Shopping, beaches, nightlife- Antalya has it all; while nearby Belek is the country's leading golf resort

A rapidly growing city of nearly a million people, Antalya is the main administrative and commercial center for most of the Turkish Mediterranean coast. The city's airport is an important gateway, receiving charter flights all year round from Europe. Sprawling around a wide bay, with the Taurus mountains as a backdrop, the city enjoys a dramatic setting.

Kaleiçi, which means "Inside the Castle", is the historic heart of the city. Surrounded by the old city walls, its narrow streets are lined with Ottoman timber-frame houses, many of which have been renovated or converted into hotels. The old harbour has been tastefully redeveloped and is surrounded by cafes, shops and restaurants. The buildings of this area enjoy official protection, so any renovation or building work is tightly controlled.

West of the center, Konyaaltı is an upmarket residential area with a long beach lined with cafes, bars and hotels. The city's other main beach and tourist area is 12 km east of the center at

ANTALYA AT A GLANCE
Population: 700,000
Telephone Area Code: 0242
Airport: Antalya (20 mins)

PROPERTY LOWDOWN
TYPICAL PRICES
Apartment (2-bed): £65,000
Villa (3-bed): £140,000
Rental Potential: Fair-Good

Advantages:
Excellent facilities and shopping
Year-round flights to UK
Large choice of property
Golfing centre

Disadvantages:
Built-up and congested
Expensive in some areas

AGENTS & DEVELOPERS
Motif Homes
Tel: 0121 2869213
www.motifhomes.com

Property-Turkey
Tel: 0871 310 9972
www.property-turkey.co.uk

Lara. The city has several huge shopping malls and a massive market.

Antalya's property market is dominated by modern apartments and prices vary hugely according to location. Two-bedroom apartments are available from £30,000 in inland districts. In Lara, however, two-bedroom apartments cost £40,000-£110,000 depending on their proximity to the sea and the quality of build and facilities.

For those in search of an Ottoman house to restore, Kaleiçi and the area of Haşım İşcan, outside the city walls, are the places to look. But it is difficult to find a bargain these days with renovated houses costing over £150,000.

Belek, 30 km east of Antalya, is Turkey's foremost golfing area, with eight courses in the area including a newly opened 27-hole course designed by Nick Faldo. Designated as a tourism development area by the government, a string of large hotels dominate the coast, blocking access to the excellent sandy beaches in some places. Behind the wooded coastal strip villa developments have sprung-up on agricultural land. Golf aside, facilities and shopping are fairly poor at the moment though things are improving quickly. The area is a property hot spot gaining growing attention from golf enthusiasts and investors from Europe and the UK. Not all properties represent value for money, so it is important to shop around and compare location, facilities and building specifications. Apartment complexes have only recently been started in the area so there are very few resale properties on the market yet. New or off-plan, two-bedroom apartments cost £45,000-£80,000; three-bedroom apartments £65,000-£90,000. There is a much larger choice of villas. Three-bedroom villas with shared pool cost £100,000-£140,000; while larger villas with private pool cost £120,000-over £235,000. Older resale villas are available from £80,000, but the construction quality is generally low and they may not make a good long-term investment. With its status as a golfing center and improving facilities, rental potential may develop, but it is poor at the moment due to competition from the many resort hotels.

> Belek is a property hot spot gaining growing attention from golf enthusiasts and investors

After a round of golf, relax on the beach in Belek

Expert View
Belek

What is special about Belek?

Its location, less than 30 minutes from Antalya international airport; its superb climate, with 300 days of sunshine a year; its long sandy Blue Flag beaches and stunning scenery and historic sites. Then there is the golf - 8 world-class courses with three more under construction and 10 more planned over the next 10 years. The first Links course in Turkey is being built 15 minutes drive from the resort. All this makes it an international golf and tourism centre - the new Algarve.

"As an official tourism development area it is attracting a lot of investment"

Why is Belek property a good investment?

Belek is at the start of a property boom. As an official tourism development area it is attracting a lot of investment. Though strict council regulations control this development, limiting building to 4 floors and 15% of any given plot, leaving 85% green.

The weather and golf create a year-round rental period. The increase in cheap flights to Antalya means people can travel more independently and more often. In the future people will be flying in for a weekend of golf the same as they do in Spain. Package holidays to the hotels are expensive for groups, so it is cost effective to rent a villa with a cook and arrange the

golf independently. So the rental chances are greater here than anywhere else on the Turkish coast.

Prices have been increasing rapidly for the last 5 years with increases of 20-30% each year. The signs are that this will continue.

Do you have any advice on choosing a location or property?

Don't buy in the Kadriye area where there are a lot of older resale properties. They are cheap but you will have endless problems with damp, poor drainage and even flooding. Buy near the river, close to the town centre and the beach.

The quality of construction has improved dramatically in the last 2 years so buy a

recently completed or an off-plan property. A lot of new developments have service cars included in the monthly maintenance fee, which provide round the clock transport to the airport, the beach or town centre.

If the property is for rental be practical and don't buy what you like yourself. Rental apartments should have at least two bathrooms. A detached or semi-detached property has a better resale value and rental potential than an apartment, so if your pocket will stretch that far then consider a three or four-bedroom villa.

Heather Kurtgil is the managing director of Motif Homes, www.motifhomes.com

Side

A popular family resort with impressive historic ruins, long sandy beaches and a good selection of property

Sitting on a peninsular, 65 km east of Antalya, Side is a popular family beach resort that has grown up beside the atmospheric remains of an ancient Roman city. The main street, lined with touristy shops, descends to a harbour overlooked by restaurants and bars. The ruins of ancient Side, including an impressive amphitheatre and the Temple of Apollo, are scattered around the centre and there is a well-stocked local museum.

However, the main attraction for thousands of European and Turkish holidaymakers are the excellent beaches. In addition to water sports, leisure activities in the area include horse riding and white water rafting. The golf courses of Belek are a 30-minute drive away, with two courses planned for the Side area itself.

Many shops and restaurants are closed during the winter, but there are supermarkets open year-round on the main highway and in the nearby town of Manavgat, which also has a weekly market. Side has a sizable expatriate community.

Due to the historic ruins around the center, development has spread along the coast to the east and west of the resort, as well as inland towards the coastal highway. High land prices mean apartment complexes are most common, though planning regulations restrict building height to four storeys. The residential area of Kemer has a lot of new apartments generally with excellent on-site facilities. Villas are becoming more common, particularly in Çolaklı, several kilometres west of the centre. There are large, well-established cooperative developments further out.

Local prices have been relatively stable over the last 12 months and there is a wide choice of property. Two-bedroom apartments are most common and cost £45,000-£80,000. The cheaper apartments are off-plan; with more expensive properties typically boasting extra space and a nice view. Three-bedroom apartments are less common and may be reduced to sell at £70,000-£90,000. Three-bedroom villas in Çolaklı cost £95,000-£150,000 off-plan; while resale houses sometimes represent good value at £50,000-£100,000. The local rental season is June to September, with weekly rates of £250 for a two-bedroom, and £350 for a three-bedroom apartment.

SIDE AT A GLANCE
Population: 17,000
Telephone Area Code: 0242
Airport: Antalya (45 mins)

PROPERTY LOWDOWN
TYPICAL PRICES
Apartment (2-bed): £65,000
Villa (3-bed): £135,000
Rental Potential: Fair

Advantages:
Easy airport access
Good beaches and activities
Good choice of property

Disadvantages:
Quiet off-season

AGENTS & DEVELOPERS
Kaya Homes
Tel: 0845 401 1111
www.kayaturkey.com

BEACH & GOLF RESIDENCE -VIP
BELEK

Excellent Golf Villas
From £ 123.000

500 meters to 27 hole NICK FALDO golf course
2500 meters to 18 hole MONTGOMERIE golf course

SUNSET BEACH RESIDENCE 6 - VIP
Konaklı - ALANYA

Fantastic Beach Front Location
From £ 61.500

letsgototurkey
construction - real estate - investment

http://www.letsgototurkey.com
info@letsgototurkey.com
Alanya - Belek / TURKEY   Tel : 00 90 242 513 20 64

Alanya

Alanya has grown into one of the largest resorts on the Turkish Mediterranean

With its beaches and year-round facilities, Alanya is a hot spot for holiday-home buyers and a growing number of retirees

Alanya is one of the largest resorts on the Turkish Mediterranean coast. Formerly the winter capital of the Selçuk Turkish empire, the modern town has grown rapidly in the shadow of a medieval castle built on a sea-girt rock which dominates the coast for miles in each direction. In addition to the historic interest of the castle and city walls, Alanya has excellent leisure facilities and good beaches, including several Blue Flag-awarded stretches. The town's lively nightlife is centered on the harbour district, where there are lots of restaurants, bars and clubs. There are also plenty of shops, supermarkets and a large weekly market.

Alanya has grown rapidly in the last 15 years with development stretching over 20 km along the coast. Particularly popular with German, Scandinavian, Dutch and Irish tourists, the number of British visitors, and property buyers, is increasing. There are 13,000 foreign-owned properties with about 9,000 permanent overseas residents, many of them retirees attracted by the area's

ALANYA AT A GLANCE
Population: 90,000
Telephone Area Code: 0242
Airport: Antalya (1.5 hours)

PROPERTY LOWDOWN
TYPICAL PRICES
Apartment (2-bed): £55,000
Villa (3-bed): £160,000
Rental Potential: Fair

Advantages:
Good beaches and facilities
Year-round community
Good choice of property

Disadvantages:
Urban setting
Poor infrastructure in some areas
Relatively few villas

Expert View
Alanya

What is special about Alanya and how does it compare to other Turkish resorts?

Alanya is one of the only Turkish resorts that is truly a year-round town. Visit many of the other resorts after the end of October and they are ghost towns, but there's a population of over 200,000 in Alanya so all the shops, restaurants and amenities stay open. The cost of living is low because of the large resident population and the quality of life is excellent. The average temperature was 25°C last December and we always have lots of winter sun. It is also a really cosmopolitan resort with an international character.

Why is property in Alanya a good investment? What is your prediction for capital growth over the next 3 years?

The demand for property does not depend on foreign buyers, as lots of Turkish people are moving into the area to find jobs and take advantage of the excellent quality of life. The new mortgage system means many more of these people will soon be able to buy their own homes, increasing demand and pushing up prices. Many of the outlying suburbs, such as Konaklı, are becoming resorts in their own right. Property prices are lower than the

"The demand for property in Alanya does not depend on foreign buyers"

centre, the infrastructure is being improved quickly and you can still find new property in prime locations. In general, I wouldn't be surprised to see increases in property values of at least 50% over the next three year, possibly a lot more in the most desirable areas.

Does the town have a viable rental market? Which areas are the best for rentals?

High-quality rental property is in short supply, particularly in the summer when the local population doubles. Long-term or seasonal lets bring in lower rates than holiday lets, but bills are paid by the tenant and there will be very little management involved. Long-term lets can produce a 5% yield. The best areas for rental property are nice residential

neighbourhoods close to the centre or in the best suburbs. Being close to the beach is always an advantage, whether you are looking for holiday lets or long-term rental and apartments on complexes with good facilities are always in demand.

Do you have any general advice for people interested in buying in Turkey?

Choose the company you deal with careful – make sure they are well established with a good track record, and they should provide a full service including after-sales and rental management.

Taylan Gündeşlioğlu is managing director of Letsgototurkey, www.letsgototurkey.com

mild winters and low cost of living.

Apartments are the most common property type with a huge number of new developments. This gives buyers a great choice, and has slowed price increases, but the resale market, particularly for older properties, is slow. In the center, most properties are resale apartments over five years old and in need of renovation. Prices start from £50,000 for a three-bedroom apartment in need of modernisation. Expect to pay £65,000-£90,000 for a new three-bedroom apartment near the beach or with a view. Apartments and houses on the lower slopes of the castle rock, which have views and greener surroundings, sell at a hefty premium.

The suburb of Cikcili, to the east of the centre, has easy access to the beach and the town center. There are a lot of new high-rise apartment complexes with excellent on-site leisure facilities. Two-bedroom apartments cost £45,000- £65,000. There are new villa developments on the mountains above the town and in the pretty Dinçay valley. Prices start from £150,000 for a three-bedroom villa with shared pool, or £160,000-£200,000 for a larger villa on a complex with good views.

Mahmutlar, 15 km east of the center, is a small but rapidly growing resort, with prices about 10% lower than Alanya. Apartment blocks have sprouted from banana plantations inland of the coastal highway in the last 6 years. The local infrastructure isn't fully established, though it is improving rapidly with the help of investment from developers. Two-bedroom apartments on a complex with shared pool range cost £45,000-£60,000.

Further east still, and 20 km from the centre of Alanya, Demirtaş also has new apartment developments and resale properties at lower prices. The municipality of Konaklı, to the west of Alanya, is an up-and-coming area with new developments fronting the sea.

Thanks to a rapidly growing permanent population and a long holiday season, Alanya's rental market has potential, although the huge supply of property makes choosing a high-quality apartment or villa in a good location essential. New three-bedroom furnished apartments typically rent for £300-£400 per week in summer, or £275-£350 per month for a long let.

AGENTS & DEVELOPERS
Flagman & Taylor
Tel: +90 5327976776
www.flagman-taylor.com

Letsgototurkey
Tel: +90 242 5132064
www.letsgototurkey.com

Mahmutlar, 15 km east of the center, is a small but rapidly growing resort

Kleopatra beach and the town's castle

A Buyer's Tale
Family Affair

Buying a property in Turkey has become more than a family affair for the Abdullas. Optometrist Nizam Abdulla has managed to persuade six of his friends to buy an apartment off-plan in the same development in Alanya. "We mix in the same social circles and our wives meet each other regularly, so we thought it was a good idea," says Nizam, who managed to persuade the developer to reserve six sea view apartments whilst he returned to the UK to speak to his friends.

Initially, he had been looking for a villa on the sea front for their retirement but couldn't find anywhere suitable. So when he was shown a development just 350 metres from the sea, he leapt at the chance. His friends did too. "I got back to England and each of my friends decided to go for an apartment too," says Nizam who lives with his wife, Rukhasna, in London's South Kensington. "We ended up buying six of the 12 apartments facing the sea." He paid €149,900 for the three-bedroom, three bathroom apartment with

"We ended up buying six of the 12 apartments facing the sea"

two balconies, which is due for completion in September 2008. Buying off-plan allowed him to make changes to the layout, including making two of the bathrooms en-suite. "We have all changed the interior in different ways as we didn't want to go into each other's apartments and know where everything is," laughs Nizam.

Facilities on the 82-apartment development include indoor and outdoor swimming pools, tennis and squash courts, a gymnasium, massage area and meeting room. "The meeting room will be very convenient as we are all in business," says Nizam, adding that service charges are expected to be around €50 a month.

He returned to Alanya in June to see the initial building work

and sign contracts. He found a Turkish solicitor through the British Consul to look over the contracts, permissions and registrations and keep an eye on the progress of the building work.

A 10% deposit has been paid and the remainder will be made in three instalments. Solicitor's fees are £1,500. Nizam says he chose Turkey because the property was reasonably priced and the economy is growing rapidly. Although the apartment has been bought mainly as an investment and for their retirement, he may also rent it out.

Nizam and Rukhasna Abdulla bought from
Flagman & Taylor,
www.flagman-taylor.com

Cappadocia & Istanbul

Cappadocia

A magical landscape and fascinating history, plus some very unusual houses, are attracting a few foreign buyers

CAPPADOCIA AT A GLANCE
Population: 350,000
Telephone Area Code: 0384
Airport: Nevşehir /Kayseri
(30 / 90 mins)

PROPERTY LOWDOWN
TYPICAL PRICES
Apartment (2-bed): N/A
Villa (3-bed): £80,000
Rental Potential: Poor

Advantages:
Beautiful landscape and
fascinating history
Unusual property
Lots of renovation projects

Disadvantages:
Major bureaucracy for renovators
Limited re-sale market

AGENTS & DEVELOPERS
Buy Cappadocia
Tel: +90 384 3416520
www.buycappadocia.com

Cappadocia is one of the country's most unusual places to buy property. Located in central Turkey, south east of the capital Ankara, the region has an amazing landscape of eroded valleys, canyons and pinnacles carved from the soft volcanic rock.

Protected within a National Park, it has a rich history and is dotted with ancient underground cities and churches. There are unsubstantiated rumours about several new golf course projects in the area. At an altitude of over 1,000m, the climate is cold and snowy in winter, with cooler summers than the coast.

Until recently, local people lived in stone houses, often burrowed from the rock. Many of these cave houses have now been abandoned or turned into hotels catering for the thousands of tourists who visit each year. A few are also being transformed into atmospheric holiday homes.

Formerly small farming communities, rural life in Göreme and Uçhisar continues alongside the tourist shops, restaurants and hotels. Cave houses in these villages are sought after and prices are relatively high, with a large renovated cave house fetching £70,000-over £100,000. The nearby village of Ortahisar has renovated houses from £50,000, or un-renovated cave houses from £20,000-£50,000. These will typically require extensive work. Renovated properties and ruins are also available in outlying villages, such as Ibrahimpaşa.

The towns of Ürgüp and Avanos have old stone houses, many of which require extensive renovation. Although less picturesque than the area's villages, they have more shops and services. The provincial town of Nevşehir and the city of Kayseri both have airports served by domestic flights from Istanbul and Ankara.

Local building regulations are tight due to the area's historic and geological importance. The best renovations retain the charming original features often found in cave houses, while incorporating modern comforts such as central heating and en-suite bathrooms. Many old houses belong to local families and prices can differ wildly from those quoted above. Properties are often sold by word-of-mouth and keen bargaining skills may be needed to get a fair price. Potential buyers should spend plenty of time exploring the area and enlist the help of a trustworthy local person or agent.

Istanbul

The city's property market is booming due to strong economic growth and a rapidly increasing population

Istanbul is the commercial, industrial and cultural heart of Turkey. The city's population is officially 12 million, though the true figure is certainly far higher, with more than 700,000 new residents arriving each year. In a city growing so quickly there is immense and growing demand for housing, though the interest rate increase in May/June 2006 put a temporary brake on the market. Rapid economic growth, dropping interest rates and the development of the recently introduced mortgage system are expected to stoke demand for housing. A growing number of foreign investors and buyers are entering the market as confidence in the country's economic stability slowly increases. Property values have risen rapidly despite an unprecedented building boom, with a recent report by the Urban Land Institute and PricewaterhouseCoopers suggesting real estate in Istanbul is now more expensive than Madrid, Rome and Stockholm. Indeed, houses in the most desirable areas of the city, such as the leafy suburbs lining the Bosphorus, command multi-million dollar price tags.

But despite rapidly rising prices, off-plan apartments are available in large suburban developments from as little as £25,000. These complexes, generally boasting excellent facilities and located close to main highways, are hugely popular with middle-class Turkish buyers and investors. There are dozens of developments in areas like Ümraniye and Ataşehir, on the Asian side of the city, or Bahçeşehir, on the European side. Prices in and around Bahçeşehir, for example, range from £500-£1,100 per m2 for apartments, townhouses or more luxurious villas at the top of the price range.

A short walk from the city centre, Cihangir is particularly popular with foreign residents. In nearby Beyoğlu and Galata, the streets off İstiklal Caddesi, the city's main shopping street, are lined with historic buildings. Formerly poor and seedy, Istanbul's answer to Soho has many renovated apartments. Expect to pay from £75,000 for a two-bedroom apartment – a lot more for a scenic roof terrace or a larger than average place. Local rental demand is strong, with monthly rates from £500 for a nice two-bedroom flat. A short distance from Beyoğlu, areas like Tarlabaşı and Kasımpaşa are rough and seedy, but prices are very low and the potential long-term returns for intrepid investors are high.

ISTANBUL AT A GLANCE
Population: 12,000,000
Telephone Area Code:
0212 (Europe) 0216 (Asia)
Airport: Atatürk Havalimanı
(20-60 mins)

PROPERTY LOWDOWN
TYPICAL PRICES
Apartment (2-bed): £90,000
Villa (3-bed): £250,000
Rental Potential: Good

Advantages:
Cosmopolitan city
Large choice of property
Excellent rental potential

Disadvantages:
Congested urban center
High prices in some areas

AGENTS & DEVELOPERS
Dream Homes Worldwide
Tel: 0800 0193847
www.dreamhomesww.com

Turkish Property People
Tel: 01622 764200
www.turkishpropertypeople.co.uk

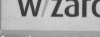

Information

PropertyIndex

A directory of currently available resale, new and off-plan property on Turkish developments

KEY
Property types

Off-plan – OP	`OP`
New – NW	`NW`
Resale – RS	`RS`
Apartments – AP	`AP`
Duplexes – DU	`DU`
Houses/Villas – HV	`HV`

Note: property prices quoted in this index may be subject to change

ALANYA
BDC Construction
`OP` `NW` `AP` `DU`
Alanya
£42,000 - £97,000
Tel: +90 5327976776
www.flagman-taylor.com

King of the Castle
`RS` `HV`
Alanya
£752,000
Tel: +90 5327976776
www.flagman-taylor.com

Lilian Heights
`OP` `NW` `AP` `DU`
Alanya
£50,500 - £123,000
Tel: +90 5327976776
www.flagman-taylor.com

Oba Beach
`NW` `AP` `DU`
Alanya, Oba
£58,000 - £102,000
Tel: +90 242 5132064
www.letsgototurkey.com

Ocean View Residence
`NW` `AP`
Alanya, Demirtaş
£49,000 - £60,500
Tel: +90 242 5132064
www.letsgototurkey.com

Ocean View Residence III
`NW` `AP` `DU`
Alanya, Cikcilli
£55,000 - £130,000
Tel: +90 242 5132064
www.letsgototurkey.com

Ocean View Residence IV
`NW` `AP` `DU`
Alanya, Kargıcak
£79,000 - £130,000
Tel: +90 242 5132064
www.letsgototurkey.com

Ocean View Residence V
`OP` `AP` `DU`
Alanya, Tepe
£95,000 - £115,000
Tel: +90 242 5132064
www.letsgototurkey.com

Seaview Penthouses
`RS` `DU`
Alanya
£143,726
Tel: +90 5327976776
www.flagman-taylor.com

Sunset Beach Residence VI
`OP` `AP` `DU`
Alanya, Konaklı
£61,500 - £130,000
Tel: +90 242 5132064
www.letsgototurkey.com

ALTINKUM/ DIDIM
Akbük Residence
`OP` `AP` `DU`
Akbük
£55,000 - £75,000
Tel: 029 20419058
www.altinkumhomes.com

Altan 2
`OP` `NW` `AP` `DU`
Altınkum
£36,500 - £55,000
Tel: +90 256 8135856
www.turkishpremierhomes.com

Alturk Grove 2
`OP` `NW` `AP` `DU`
Altınkum
£40,500 - £57,000
Tel: +90 256 8135856
www.turkishpremierhomes.com

Alturk Grove 3
`OP` `NW` `AP` `DU`
Altınkum
£26,000 - £60,000
Tel: +90 256 8135856
www.turkishpremierhomes.com

Apollonium
`OP` `NW` `AP` `HV`
Didim
£71,900 - £112,400
Tel: 0800 0193847
www.dreamhomesww.com

Aydin Villas
`NW` `HV`
Akbük
£110,000 - £130,000
Tel: 029 20419058
www.altinkumhomes.com

Blue City
`NW` `DU` `HV`
Didim
£60,000 - £110,000
Tel: 029 20419058
www.altinkumhomes.com

Boyd Villas
`OP` `NW` `HV`
Altınkum
£85,000
Tel: +90 256 8135856
www.turkishpremierhomes.com

Celikoglu
`NW` `HV`
Altınkum
£65,000
Tel 01772735151
www.turkishconnextions.co.uk

Cornellia Village 2
`NW` `AP` `DU`
Altınkum
£39,900 - £57,500
Tel: 0207 6241782
www.solmet.co.uk

Golden Beach
`NW` `RS` `HV`
Altınkum
£140,000
Tel 01772735151
www.turkishconnextions.co.uk

Mayfair Luxury Apartments II
`OP` `AP` `DU`
Altınkum
£24,990 - £49,990
Tel: 0207 6241782
www.solmet.co.uk

Medusa Village
`NW` `HV`
Altınkum
£95,000
Tel: +90 256 8135856
www.turkishpremierhomes.com

Get expert help with your Turkish property hunt at:
www.buyingin.co.uk

Mimosa Apartments
`OP` `NW` `AP` `DU`
Altınkum
£35,000 - £58,000
Tel 01772735151
www.turkishconnextions.co.uk

Onder Villas
`NW` `HV`
Altınkum
£120,000
Tel 01772735151
www.turkishconnextions.co.uk

Orista Gardens
`RS` `AP`
Altınkum
£46,000
Tel 01772735151
www.turkishconnextions.co.uk

Papatya Apartments
`OP` `AP` `DU`
Altınkum, Didim
£40,000 - £70,000
Tel: 029 20419058
www.altinkumhomes.com

Sanctuary Villas
NW **HV**
Mavişehir, Didim
£130,000 - £150,000
Tel: 029 20419058
www.altinkumhomes.com

Sea Garden
NW **AP** **DU**
Altınkum
£47,000 - £75,000
Tel: 0207 6241782
www.solmet.co.uk

The Sun Complex 2
OP **NW** **AP** **DU**
Altınkum
£41,000 - £70,000
Tel 01772735151
www.turkishconnextions.co.uk

Thalia
OP **AP** **DU**
Altınkum
£37,000 - £57,000
Tel: 0207 6241782
www.solmet.co.uk

Topaz Residence
OP **AP**
Altınkum
£19,999 - £30,000
Tel: 0207 6241782
www.solmet.co.uk

ANTALYA & BELEK
Motif Apartments PT278
NW **AP**
Belek
£40,000 - £60,000
Tel: +90 242 7537175
www.motifhomes.com

Motif Apartments PT332
OP **AP** **DU**
Belek
£67,000 - £110,000
Tel: +90 242 7537175
www.motifhomes.com

Motif Belek Apartments MH272
OP **AP** **DU**
Belek
£65,000 - £75,000
Tel: +90 242 7537175
www.motifhomes.com

Motif Golf Aparts PT279
OP **AP**
Belek
£65,000 - £75,000
Tel: +90 242 7537175
www.motifhomes.com

Golf View Villas MH284
NW **HV**
Belek
£160,000 - £260,000
Tel: +90 242 7537175
www.motifhomes.com

Motif Golf Villas PT283
OP **HV**
Belek
£130,000 - £140,000
Tel: +90 242 7537175
www.motifhomes.com

Mountain View Apartments MH338
OP **AP** **DU**
Belek
£49,000 - £89,000
Tel: +90 242 7537175
www.motifhomes.com

Oceanfront Antalya
OP **NW** **AP**
Lara beach, Antalya
£68,500 - £89,000
Tel: +90 5327976776
www.flagman-taylor.com

Pegasus Court
OP **NW** **AP**
Antalya
£53,000 - £64,000
Tel 01772735151
www.turkishconnextions.co.uk

Riverside Apartments PT273
OP **AP** **DU**
Belek
£80,000 - £120,000
Tel: +90 242 7537175
www.motifhomes.com

Villas Motif PT331
OP **HV**
Belek
£100,000 - £110,000
Tel: +90 242 7537175
www.motifhomes.com

BODRUM
Beach Park
OP **AP**
Yalıkavak, Bodrum
£62,500 - £92,500
Tel: 01202 887369
www.harmonyhomesbodrum.com

Bluewater Villas
OP **NW** **HV**
Küçübük
£99,000 - £160,000
Tel: 0800 0193847
www.dreamhomesww.com

Bostanci Villas
OP **NW** **HV**
Yalıkavak
£170,000
Tel: 0800 0193847
www.dreamhomesww.com

Deep Valley
`OP` `AP` `DU` `HV`
Yalıkavak, Bodrum
£58,000 - £170,000
Tel: 01202 887369
www.harmonyhomesbodrum.com

Dolphin Apartments
`NW` `AP`
Gümüşlük, Bodrum
£73,000 - £78,000
Tel: 01202 887369
www.harmonyhomesbodrum.com

Gaia 2
`NW` `AP`
Yalıkavak, Bodrum
£55,000
Tel: 01772735151
www.turkishconnections.co.uk

Harmony Beach
`OP` `AP`
Gümüşlük, Bodrum
£49,000 - £79,000
Tel: 01202 887369
www.harmonyhomesbodrum.com

Luxury Detached Villas
`NW` `HV`
Bodrum
£144,900 - £270,000
Tel: +90 256 6131770
www.turkeyexpert.co.uk

Olive Tree Villas
`OP` `NW` `HV`
Güllük
£139,700
Tel: 0800 0193847
www.dreamhomesww.com

Opus Beach Houses
`OP` `NW` `AP`
Gündoğan
£64,000 - £184,000
Tel: 0800 0193847
www.dreamhomesww.com

Sea View Regency Prestige
`NW` `HV`
Gündoğan, Bodrum
£181,000 - £196,000
Tel: +90 252 3191897
www.cumberland-properties.com

Sunset Bay
`OP` `NW` `AP`
Güllük
£61,000 - £88,900
Tel: 0800 0193847
www.dreamhomesww.com

Turquoise
`OP` `NW` `AP`
Bodrum
£62,500 - £79,400
Tel: 0800 0193847
www.dreamhomesww.com

Turquoise Bay Complex
`OP` `NW` `AP` `DU`
Tuzla, Bodrum
£53,000 - £95,000
Tel: 01772735151
www.turkishconnextions.co.uk

Valley Gardens Regency
`OP` `AP`
Gökçebel, Bodrum
£120,000 - £140,500
Tel: +90 252 3191897
www.cumberland-properties.com

Woodland Regency
`OP` `AP` `HV`
Konacık, Bodrum
£54,500 - £170,500
Tel: +90 252 3191897
www.cumberland-properties.com

Yalıkavak Hills
`NW` `AP` `DU`
Yalıkavak, Bodrum
£68,000 - £99,000
Tel: 01202 887369
www.harmonyhomesbodrum.com

ÇEŞME
Aegean View Villas
`OP` `NW` `HV`
Çiftlikköy, Çeşme
£114,000 - £125,000
Tel: +90 536 4613512
www.villasinturkey.net

Majestic Villas
`RS` `HV`
Çiftlikköy, Çeşme
£120,000
Tel: +90 536 4613512
www.villasinturkey.net

The Olive Grove
`OP` `NW` `HV`
Çeşme
£117,000 - £125,000
Tel: +90 536 4613512
www.villasinturkey.net

Regal Villas
`OP` `NW` `HV`
Çiftlikköy, Çeşme
£88,000 - £95,000
Tel: +90 536 4613512
www.villasinturkey.net

Sea View Villas
`OP` `NW` `HV`
Çiftlikköy, Çeşme
£120,000 - £130,000
Tel: +90 536 4613512
www.villasinturkey.net

DALAMAN
Belle Vista Villas
`OP` `HV`
Dalaman
£60,000 - £70,000
Tel: +90 252 6925398
www.dalamanturkishvillas.com

Belle Vista Apartments
NW AP
Dalaman
£47,500 - £48,500
Tel: +90 252 6925398
www.dalamanturkishvillas.com

Florya Villas
NW HV
Dalaman
£99,950
Tel: +90 252 6925398
www.dalamanturkishvillas.com

Flower Homes Apartments
NW AP
Dalaman
£40,000
Tel: +90 252 6925398
www.dalamanturkishvillas.com

The Hills
OP HV
Akkaya, Dalaman
£132,000 - £158,000
Tel: 0845 355 5625
www.curbanoglu.co.uk

Lakeside Villas
OP HV
Akkaya, Dalaman
£79,000
Tel: 0845 355 5625
www.curbanoglu.co.uk

The Links/Artemis Project
OP AP DU HV
Sarıgerme, Dalaman
£80,000 - £128,000
Tel: 01282 446035
www.propertyinturkey.com

Ottoman Village
NW HV
Dalaman
£99,000
Tel: 0845 355 5625
www.curbanoglu.co.uk

Venus Apartments
OP NW AP DU
Sarıgerme, Dalaman
£95,000 - £100,000
Tel: 01282 446035
www.propertyinturkey.com

Whiterock Bungalows
OP HV
Akkaya, Dalaman
£108,000
Tel: 0845 355 5625
www.curbanoglu.co.uk

Whiterock Villas
NW HV
Akkaya, Dalaman
£154,000
Tel: 0845 355 5625
www.curbanoglu.co.uk

DALYAN
Club Waner
NW AP
Dalyan
£45,000
Tel: +90 252 2843946
www.niobeproperty.com

Ebru Apartments
NW AP
Dalyan
£45,000
Tel: +90 252 2843946
www.niobeproperty.com

May Apartments
NW AP
Dalyan
£45,000
Tel: +90 252 2843946
www.niobeproperty.com

Güllü Residence
OP HV
Dalyan,
£72,500 - £139,000
Tel: +90 242 3242219
www.euromedt-turkey.com

The Onyx
NW AP DU HV
Dalyan
£39,000 - £126,500
Tel: 01282 446035
www.propertyinturkey.com

Niobe Villas
NW HV
Dalyan
£95,000 - £115,000
Tel: +90 252 2843946
www.niobeproperty.com

Zircon Apartments
NW AP DU
Dalyan
£68,000
Tel: 01282 446035
www.propertyinturkey.com

FETHIYE
Amber Apartments
NW AP DU
Ovacık, Fethiye
£66,000
Tel: 01282 446035
www.propertyinturkey.com

The Aqua Villa
NW HV
Ovacık, Fethiye
£129,000
Tel: 01282 446035
www.propertyinturkey.com

The Dell Villa and Apart
NW AP HV
Ovacık, Fethiye
£139,000
Tel: 01282 446035
www.propertyinturkey.com

Design Your Own
OP HV
Üzümlü, Fethiye
£120,000
Tel: 01282 446035
www.propertyinturkey.com

Flamingo Apartments
AP
Çalış Beach, Fethiye
£85,000 - £165,000
Tel: +90 252 6132377
www.taureanproperties.co.uk

Harbour Heights
OP AP
Fethiye
£70,000 - £150,000
Tel: +90 252 6132377
www.taureanproperties.co.uk

Lagoon Villas
HV
Ovacık, Ölüdeniz
£139,000 - £145,000
Tel: +90 252 6132377
www.taureanproperties.co.uk

Lara Apartments
NW AP
Fethiye
£40,000 - £43,000
Tel: 01282 446035
www.propertyinturkey.com

Lemon 6
AP
Çalış Beach, Fethiye
£35,000 - £45,000
Tel: +90 252 6132377
www.taureanproperties.co.uk

Seabreeze Villas
HV
Çalış Beach, Fethiye
£110,000
Tel: +90 252 6132377
www.taureanproperties.co.uk

KALKAN
Breeze Villas
NW HV
Kalkan
£169,000 - £179,000
Tel: +90 5322612296
www.kalkanproperty.com

Club Patara Villas
RS HV
Kalkan
£179,000 - £400,000
Tel: +90 5322612296
www.kalkanproperty.com

Kalamar Sun Apartments
NW AP DU
Kalkan
£72,000 - £82,000
Tel: +90 5322612296
www.kalkanproperty.com

Kalamar Bay Villas
NW RS HV
Kalkan
£199,000 - £400,000
Tel: +90 5322612296
www.kalkanproperty.com

Kisla Deluxe Villas
NW HV
Kalkan
£179,000 - £225,000
Tel: +90 5322612296
www.kalkanproperty.com

Mavi Duplex Apartments
NW AP DU
Kalkan
£79,000 - £89,000
Tel: +90 5322612296
www.kalkanproperty.com

Mina Apartments
NW AP DU
Kalkan
£95,000 - £115,000
Tel:+90 5322612296
www.kalkanproperty.com

Ocean Duplex Apartments
OP AP DU
Kalkan
£107,500
Tel: +90 5322612296
www.kalkanproperty.com

Olivia Villas
OP HV
Kalkan
£215,000 - £270,000
Tel: +90 533 4273208
www.myturkishproperty.com

Yelken Villas
NW HV
Kalkan
£185,000
Tel: +90 5322612296
www.kalkanproperty.com

Zeus Villas
NW HV
Kalkan
£180,000 - £195,000
Tel: +90 5322612296
www.kalkanproperty.com

KAŞ
The Hillside Apartments
OP NW AP DU
Kaş
£50,000 - £132,000
Tel: +90 533 4273208
www.myturkishproperty.com

Olive Grove Cottages
OP HV
Bayındır, Kaş
£100,000 - £130,000
Tel: +90 533 4273208
www.myturkishproperty.com

The Seafront Apartments
NW AP
Kas Peninsula, Kaş
£145,000
Tel: +90 533 4273208
www.myturkishproperty.com

Turkuaz Villas
NW RS
Kaş Peninsula, Kaş
£225,000 - £280,000
Tel: +90 533 4273208
www.myturkishproperty.com

KUŞADASI
City Apartments
NW AP
Kuşadası
£50,500 - £119,000
Tel: +90 256 6131770
www.turkeyexpert.co.uk

Club Oliva
OP NW AP DU
Kuşadası
£55,000 - £145,000
Tel: +90 535 2155265
www.propertyofturkey.com

Karaova Villas
OP NW HV
Long Beach, Kuşadası
£109,000 - £142,500
Tel: 01293 422305
www.capitaldevelopments.net

Lemon Grove
OP NW AP DU HV
Ladies Beach, Kuşadası
£50,000 - £109,000
Tel: 01293 422305
www.capitaldevelopments.net

Magnolia Apartment
OP AP
Ladies Beach, Kuşadası
£57,800 - £95,200
Tel: +90 256 6131770
www.turkeyexpert.co.uk

Mediterranean Villas
NW HV
Kuşadası
£132,500 - £153,000
Tel: +90 256 6131770
www.turkeyexpert.co.uk

Oliva Hanya Villas
NW HV
Long Beach, Kuşadası
£95,000 - £120,000
Tel: +90 535 2155265
www.propertyofturkey.com

Oliva Residence
NW AP DU
Kuşadası
£95,000 - £165,000
Tel: +90 535 2155265
www.propertyofturkey.com

Oliva Villas
NW HV
Kuşadası
£169,500 - £245,000
Tel: +90 535 2155265
www.propertyofturkey.com

Olive Grove
RS AP DU HV
Ladies Beach, Kuşadası
£60,500 - £114,000
Tel: 01293 422305
www.capitaldevelopments.net

Ozdere Apartments
NW AP
Ozdere
£25,350 - £46,900
Tel: +90 256 6131770
www.turkeyexpert.co.uk

Ponz Villas
RS HV
Ladies Beach, Kuşadası
£62,000 - £72,000
Tel: 01293 422305
www.capitaldevelopments.net

Walnut Grove
OP NW HV
Soğucak, Kuşadası
£95,000 - £112,000
Tel: 01293 422305
www.capitaldevelopments.net

Waterfall Apartments
NW AP DU
Kuşadası
Tel: +90 535 2155265
www.propertyofturkey.com

SIDE
Motif Villas PT109
OP HV
Side
£100,000 - £120,000
Tel: +90 242 7537175
www.motifhomes.com

Oasis Residence
OP AP
£55,000 - £135,000
Tel: 0845 401 1111
www.kayaturkey.com

Directory

PROPERTY NEWS & ONLINE GUIDES AT WWW.BUYINGINGUIDES.INFO

AIRLINES & TRAVEL
Alternative Travel
Tel: 08700 411448
www.alternativeturkey.com

British Airways
Tel: 0870 8509850
www.ba.com

EasyJet
www.Easyjet.com

Sun Express
Tel: 0845 6001521
www.sunexpress.com.tr

Turkish Airlines
Tel: 0207 7669300
www.thy.com.tr

Turkish Cyprus Airlines
Tel: 0207 9304851
www.kthy.net

AIRLINES (CHARTER)
Avro
Tel: 0870 4582841
www.avro.co.uk

Excel
Tel: 0870 1690169
www.xl.com

Holidays 4U
Tel: 0870 444 2840
www.holidays-4u.co.uk

MyTravel
Tel: 0870 238 7777
www.mytravel.com

Thomas Cook
Tel: 08707505711
www.thomascook.com

AIRLINES (DOMESTIC)
Atlas Jet
Tel: +90 216 4440387
www.atlasjet.com/eng

Flyair
Tel: +90 212 4444359
www.flyair.com.tr

Onur Air
Tel: +90 212 6629797
www.onurair.com.tr

Pegasus
Tel: +90 444 0737
www.flypgs.com

Sun Express
Tel: 0845 6001521
www.sunexpress.com.tr

ASSOCIATIONS
Association of International Property Professionals
Tel: 020 74097061
www.aipp.org.uk

Federation of Overseas Developers Agents & Consultants
Tel: 0870 3501223
www.fopdac.com

BANKS
Finansbank
Tel: +90 444 0900
www.finansbank.com.tr

Garanti Bank
Tel: +90 444 0333
www.garantibank.com

Yapı ve Kredi
Tel: +90 444 0444
www.yapikredi.com/en

BUS COMPANIES
Ulusoy
Tel: +90 444 8999
www.ulusoy.com.tr/eng/

Varan
Tel: +90 444 1888
www.varan.com.tr

Get expert help with your Turkish property hunt at:
www.buyingin.co.uk

CAR RENTAL
Avis
Tel: +90 212 3686800
www.avis.com.tr

Bougainville Turizm
Tel: +90 242 836 3737
www.bougainville-turkey.com

Real Tours/Europcar
Tel: +90 252 6144995
www.realtour.com.tr

Sixt
Tel: +90 212 3189040
www.sunrent.com

COURIER COMPANIES
Aras
Tel: +90 216 5385555
www.araskargo.com/en/

UPS
Tel: +90 212 4440033
www.ups.com.tr

Turkish Premier Homes
Tel: +90 256 8135856
www.turkishpremierhomes.com

Villas in Turkey
Tel: +90 536 4613512
www.villasinturkey.net

AGENTS & DEVELOPERS
West Mediterranean:
Marmaris, Dalaman, Fethiye,
Kalkan, Kaş
Curbanoglu
Tel: 0845 355 5625
www.curbanoglu.co.uk

Dalaman Turkish Villas
Tel: +90 252 6925398
www.dalamanturkishvillas.com

Lycia Properties
Tel: 01282 446035
www.propertyinturkey.com

Mavi Estates
Tel: +90 5322612296
www.kalkanproperty.com

Niobe Properties
Tel: +90 252 2843946
www.niobeproperty.com

Tandem Villas
Tel: +90 242 8363287
www.tandemvillas.com

Taurean Properties
Tel: +90 252 6132377
www.taureanproperties.co.uk

Turquaz Emlak
Tel: +90 533 4273208
www.myturkishproperty.com

AGENTS & DEVELOPERS
East Mediterranean: Antalya,
Side, Alanya
Euromedt
Tel: +90 242 3242219
www.euromedt-turkey.com

AGENTS & DEVELOPERS
Aegean: Ayvalık, Çeşme,
Altınkum, Kuşadası, Bodrum
Altinkum Homes
Tel: 029 20419058
www.altinkumhomes.com

Capital Developments
Tel: 01293 422 305
www.capitaldevelopments.net

Cumberland Properties
Tel: +90 252 3191897
www.cumberland-properties.com

Dream Homes Worldwide
Tel: 0800 0193 847
www.dreamhomesww.com

Harmony Homes
Tel: 01202 887369
www.harmonyhomesbodrum.com

Property of Turkey
Tel: +90 535 2155265
www.propertyofturkey.com

Seaside Properties
Tel: +90 252 3637191
www.seasidepropertiesturkey.com

Solmet
Tel: 0207 6241782
www.solmet.co.uk

Turkey Expert
Tel: +90 256 6131770
www.turkeyexpert.co.uk

Turkish Connextions
Tel: 01772 735151
www.turkishconnextions.co.uk

Flagman & Taylor
Tel: +90 532 797 6776
www.flagman-taylor.com

Kaya Homes
Tel: 0845 401 1111
www.kayaturkey.com

Letsgototurkey
Tel: +90 242 5132064
www.letsgototurkey.com

Motif Homes
Tel: +90 242 7537175
www.motifhomes.com

Property-Turkey.co.uk
Tel: 0871 3109972
www.property-turkey.co.uk

AGENTS & DEVELOPERS
Istanbul
Ant Yapı
Tel: 0216 4560722
www.antyapi.com

Remax
Tel: 0212 2433333
www.remax.com.tr

FOREIGN CURRENCY
DEALERS
Travelex
Tel: 0870 0100095
www.travelex.c.uk

HEALTHCARE
International Hospital
(Istanbul)
Tel: 0212 6633000
www.internationalhospital.com.tr

Eczacıbaşı Sağlık Hizmetleri
Tel 0212 3172500
www.eczacibasi.com.tr

Esnaf Hastanesi (Fethiye)
Tel: 0252 6126400
www.esnafhastanesi.com

Medicus Clinic (Side)
Tel: 0242 753111
www.medicus.com.tr

INSURANCE (TURKEY)
Anadolu Sigorta
www.anadolusigorta.com.tr

AxaOyak
www.axaoyak.com.tr

KITCHENS, FURNISHINGS & ELECTRICAL
Arçelik
Tel: 4440888
www.arcelik.com.tr

Beko
Tel: 0212 2524900
www.beko.com.tr

Bellona
Tel: 0800 361 89 86
www.bellona.com.tr

CK Yapı Dekorasyon
Tel: 0216 5419611
www.ckyapi.com.tr

IKEA
www.ikea.com.tr

İpek Mobilya
Tel: 0352 3220050
www.ipekmobilya.com.tr

Kelebek
Tel: 0216 4467715
www.kelebek.com.tr

Mudo Concept Stores
Tel: 0212 2852390
www.mudo.com.tr

LANGUAGE SCHOOLS
Dilmer
Tel: 0212 2929696
www.dilmer.com

Tömer
Tel: 0232 4640544
www.tomer.ankara.edu.
tr/english/

OFFICIAL (UK)
Turkish Consulate (London)
Tel: 020 75916900
www.turkishconsulate.org.uk

Turkish Embassy (Customs info)
Tel: 020 72456318

Turkish Tourist Office
Tel: 0207 6297771
www.gototurkey.com

OFFICIAL (TURKEY)
Turkish Embassy
Tel 0312 4553344
www.britishembassy.org.tr

Ministry of Foreign Affairs (Visa information)
www.mfa.gov.tr/MFA/
ConsularInfo
rmation/ForForeigners/

Turkish Touring & Automobile Association
Tel: +90 212 2828140
www.turing.org.tr

PRIVATE MEDICAL INSURANCE
(see also: Insurance)

AXA PPP Healthcare
Tel: 0800 121345
www.axappphealthcare.co.uk

BUPA International
Tel: 01273 208181
www.bupa-intl.com

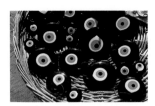

ExpaCare Insurance Services
Tel: 01344 381650
www.expacare.net

PROPERTY MANAGEMENT & RENTAL
AA Villa Renters Turkey
Tel: +90 252 6136782
www.villarentersturkey.com

Windsor Property Management
Tel: +90 252 6133585
www.alanya-answers.com

SOLICITORS
For a list of Turkish solicitors visit the Consular Services section of the British Embassy website:
www.britishembassy.org.tr

Acacia International
Tel: 0845 3670137
www.acacia-int.com

Kevin Hood
Anglo-Turkish Law Consultant
Tel: 0536 5246995

TRANSPORT FIRMS
Crown Relocations
Tel: 0113 3851000
www.cronrelo.com

Robinsons International
Tel: 01235 552266
www.robinsons-intl.com

Sumerman International Moving
Tel: +90 212 2235818
www.sumerman.com

UsefulWebsites

PROPERTY NEWS & FREE ONLINE GUIDES AT WWW.BUYINGINGUIDES.INFO

www.aegeanworld.com
Aegean resorts information site

www.alanya.cc
Alanya information

www.altinkum.com
Altınkum information website

www.antalya-ws.com
Antalya information site

www.bodrumforum.co.uk
Bodrum forum

www.bodrumlife.com
Bodrum information portal

www.buyingin.co.uk
Impartial property advice service

www.buyinginguides.info
Property information site where you can order this book

www.calis-beach.co.uk
Çalış information & forum

www.cornucopia.net
Cornucopia magazine website

www.datcainfo.com
Datça information

www.dalyan.co.uk
Dalyan information

www.fethiye.net
Fethiye information

www.gofethiye.com
Fethiye information

www.gocek.info
Göcek information

www.ido.com.tr
Online booking and times for Istanbul ferries

www.internationaleducationmedia.com/ turkey
A list of Turkish universities

www.kalkan.org.tr
Kalkan local site

www.kilim.com
Buy a Turkish carpet online

Get expert help with your Turkish property hunt at:
www.buyingin.co.uk

www.kusadasi.net
Information site about the resort

www.letsgoturkey.com
Turkey information site

www.marmaris.org
Marmaris news and information

www.marmarisinfo.com
Marmaris information site

www.mymerhaba.com
Expat network & resource

www.oliveoilturkey.com
Website about Turkish olive oil

www.theguideturkey.com
Online and print guides to Istanbul, Antalya, Bodrum and other cities

www.timeout.com.tr
Istanbul nightlife magazine

www.travelturkeymag.com
Travel features and information

www.turkeytravelplanner.com
Practical travel information

www.turkishculture.org
Turkish Cultural site

www.turkishdailynews.com
Website of Turkey's English language newspaper

www.turkey-news.com
News about Turkey from the world's press

www.turkishpress.com
News portal with Turkish & international news

www.turunc.com
Turunç resort information

www.turkishwinetours.com
Turkish wine-tasting tours